MUHAMMAD ALI

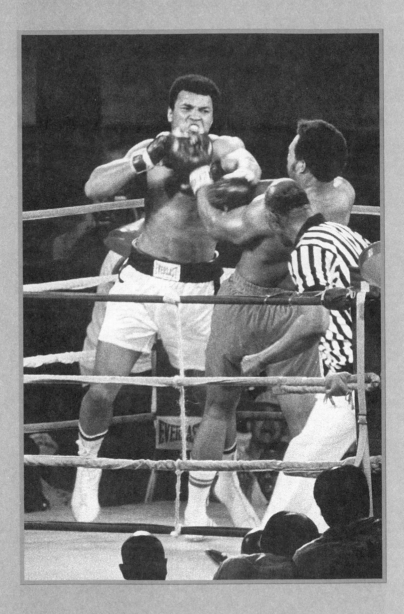

MUHAMMAD ALI

John Stravinsky

A Balliett & Fitzgerald Book

PARK LANE PRESS

PARK LANE

NEW YORK

This 1997 edition is published by Park Lane Press,
a division of Random House Value Publishing, Inc.,
a Random House Company
201 East 50th Street, New York, New York 10022

A&E's acclaimed BIOGRAPHY series is available on video cassette
from A&E Home Video. Call 1-800-423-1212 to order.

A&E and **BIOGRAPHY** are trademarks of A&E Television Networks,
registered in the United States and other countries.

Park Lane Press and colophon are trademarks of
Random House Value Publishing, Inc.

Random House
New York • Toronto • London • Sydney • Auckland
http://www.randomhouse.com/

Printed and bound in the United States of America

Quotes from Thomas Hauser: Reprinted with the permission of Simon & Schuster
from *Muhammad Ali: His Life and Times* by Thomas Hauser.
Copyright ©1991 by Thomas Hauser and Muhammad Ali

A Balliett & Fitzgerald Book
Series Editor: Thomas Dyja
Book Design: Lisa Govan, Susan Canavan
Photo Research: Maria Fernandez
Copy Editor: William Drennan
and special thanks to Judy Capadanno, Bill Huelster,
and John Groton at Random House

Library of Congress Cataloging-in-Publication Data

Stravinsky, John.
    Muhammad Ali : Biography / John Stravinsky.
        p.   cm.   —(Biographies from A&E)
    Includes bibliographical references (p.).
        1. Ali, Muhammad, 1942-   . 2. Boxers (Sports)—United States—
    Biography.   I. Title.   II. Series.
    GV1132.A44S87 1997
    796.8'3'092—dc20
    (B)   96-36218
                                                              CIP

    ISBN 0-517-20080-5
    10 9 8 7 6 5 4 3 2 1
    First Edition

CONTENTS

Rudy, left, and Cassius

CHAPTER ONE

LOUISVILLE

On April 28, 1967, the most important day of Muhammad Ali's life, the heavyweight champion sat in a Houston hotel coffee shop eating soft-boiled eggs, musing on his predicament as the nation's most famous draft dodger. "The people know the only way I can lose my title is in the ring," he said, wary of impending exile. "My title goes where I go. But if they won't let me fight it could cost me $10 million in earnings. Does that sound like I'm serious about my religion?"

As the eleventh hour approached, the time when Ali would ostensibly have to make up his mind whether to go off into the armed forces or not, many people continued to question his sincerity. What few doubted was that Ali would refuse induction. From the day over a year earlier when he had avowed, "I ain't got no quarrel with them Vietcong," Ali left little doubt about his intentions to refuse service. It remained to be seen what the

U.S. government would do (the Selective Service had denied his appeal for conscientious objector status on religious grounds as a Muslim minister).

The night before, Ali had been up chattering away with his sidekick Bundini Brown until 2:00 A.M., working off nervous energy. It was like the night before a fight, and the champ needed to exhaust himself before he could fall out. At the crack of dawn he had been up, as if ready for roadwork. He had showered, dressed in a blue suit, and waited for his lawyers to accompany him to the induction center at the U.S. Customs House on San Jacinto Street.

There was a crush of photographers and reporters on hand to greet Ali at the induction center; they would later be joined by a gaggle of protesters, a few of whom would take the occasion to burn their draft cards. Inside the building, Ali went through a battery of physical tests, joking with the other twenty-five inductees. All but Ali brought an overnight bag with their personal belongings, since they planned to leave on the 6:00 P.M. bus for Fort Polk, Louisiana. At noon, Ali wolfed everything in his box lunch but his ham sandwich.

A little after one o'clock, Ali was called with the others into the "ceremony room." Upon hearing "Cassius Marcellus Clay" called, he refused three times to step forward and was taken down the hall to a separate office, where he confirmed his refusal in writing. (He would eventually go before a federal grand jury for his actions.) Ali then proceeded to the media room, where he handed out a statement that read in part, "It is in light of my own personal convictions that I take my stand in rejecting the call to be inducted into the armed services. I do so with full realization of its implications and possible consequences. I have searched my conscience, and find I cannot be true to my belief in my religion by accepting such a call."

Ali would suffer greatly for taking the high moral ground. Facing a five-year jail sentence and a lockout from professional boxing, he could easily have faded from the picture. But how could anyone know back then that the forced exile was merely downtime in the epic career of sport's all-time greatest performer? History would eventually record Muhammad Ali as a man of many finest hours, but none would so define him as that gray April day in Houston.

❧ ❧ ❧

"Oh, he was an unusual child all his life."

The births of legendary figures are often embellished over the years by proud parents who, with hindsight, just knew on the spot that here was history being made. So it was that Cassius Marcellus Clay, Sr., would recall his firstborn, Cassius, Jr., coming into the world "with a good body and a big head that was the image of Joe Louis." Clay, Sr., also liked to point out the significance of Jr.'s first words, "Gee Gee"—how they were surely a sign that the boy was destined to win the Golden Gloves.

Officially, Cassius Marcellus Clay, Jr., weighed in at six pounds, seven ounces at 6:35 A.M. on January 17, 1942, at Louisville General Hospital—his first public appearance on record. Ali's mother, Odessa Grady Clay, would often recall the confusion of that day, something about the wrong child being wheeled around. An alert nurse quickly made the proper switch, and the real deal was soon cuddled up at bedside, wailing away. While still an infant, the future heavyweight champion would loosen one of his mother's front teeth with a straight right—again a fistic omen, the father would say.

Mrs. Clay herself would insist over the years that hers was an active child. "He'd walk way up on his toes," she once told an interviewer. "He didn't quit that tippin' till he was five years old. Oh, he was an unusual child all his life." And when the doting mother would later add that the future Louisville Lip had chattered away in his crib, had talked at a mere ten months, no one dared contest her version.

Accounts vary as to the quality of Cassius Clay's childhood and adolescence. The exaggerated picture often painted of a middle-class upbringing relies generally on the existence of a nice house, toys, family values, and such. (There was a pet chicken, a dog, an electric train set, and, until it was stolen, a much-heralded Schwinn bicycle.) Yet this clashes with Ali's own recollections of a "semipoverty" that included busted toilets, secondhand clothes, and no money for bus fare. Somewhere in between it can safely be drawn that Cassius and his younger brother Rudy were relatively comfortable and happy growing up. As Ali once summed it: "Our people were poor financially, but we was rich with health, rich with friends."

The Louisville Clays—Cassius's cousins, aunts, uncles, and all—were an enormous clan, a widespread cross section of a proud and successful line. Their many family gatherings provided a fertile breeding ground for the showmanship of a precocious child. At these festive weekend get-togethers, the gregarious young Cassius was already in his element, mixing with cousins, getting fussed over by aunts and grandmothers, and generally carrying on in the formative ways of one who would be greatest.

"My family were really happy, lively people," Ali would one day recall, "no fights, no divorces, no throwing things around.

People who have a prejudice against me have tried to harm me by saying that my childhood was full of family troubles and saying so in print. I just know I had a nice time as a kid."

To his credit, Ali has generally spoken glowingly and loyally about the solid parenting he received. But Louisville police records show that things weren't always peaceful in the Clay household. Clay, Sr., was arrested four times for reckless driving, twice for disorderly conduct, and twice for assault and battery. Three times complaints were filed by Odessa Clay after her husband had allegedly beaten her.

Clay's father was a hardworking man with a weakness for booze. Whatever tiffs did occur—and Ali has always said none did—they happened, according to friends and family, after the bottle had taken its toll. Clay, Sr., was a talented artist who in a perfect world might have had a career as such. As it was, he provided for the family as a self-employed sign painter; his handiwork would continue to be found scattered around the Louisville landscape well after his son's fame.

Clay's mother was a warm homemaker who supplemented the family income by cleaning and cooking for white households across town. (The head of one of these families, Vertner de Garno Smith, would one day take part in the syndicate that sponsored Ali in his first years as a professional.) The parents were always proud of their two well-mannered sons. Cursing was prohibited, clean clothes were a must, and attendance at a nearby Methodist church was regular. It's a testament to how well the Clays provided that, aside from sometimes helping their father paint signs, the boys hardly worked at all in their youth. Their father liked to say that "eating and sleeping" were their hardest work.

Like son, like father. An enigmatic figure, Cassius Clay, Sr., was a compulsive talker—a braggart given to inventive flights

❖ CLAY FAMILY ❖

CLAY WITH HIS
YOUNGER
BROTHER RUDY,
LEFT.

As a Black Muslim, Cassius Clay/Muhammad Ali would understandably want to rid himself of his "slave name." The birth name, after his father's, actually owes its provenance to Cassius Marcellus Clay, a gentleman abolitionist of nineteenth-century Kentucky. It is not known whether this namesake was a distant ancestor. Nor is there any proof, despite some family claims, that the Clays were descended from Henry Clay, the famous senator and presidential candidate from Kentucky. All four of Ali's grandparents were registered as "free colored" on census rolls, and it's more than likely that their forebears were slaves.

As to the maternal line, one of Clay's great-grandparents, Tom Morehead, was the son of a white man and a slave named Dinah. The other side traces back to one Abram Grady, a white Irish immigrant who married a "free colored woman" of unknown name. However blurred the genealogical branches, there are indications that one of Ali's ancestral relatives on his mother's side may have fought in the Civil War and that others were part of a group of liberated slaves who returned to Africa.

Whatever his own actual genealogical background, once Muhammad Ali had become knowledgeable in African-American history, he was very clear in his attitude toward any existence of white forefathers on his paternal side. "If slaveholder [Henry] Clay's blood came into our veins along with the name," he wrote in his 1975 autobiography *The Greatest*, "it came by rape and defilement." As he had once expounded to a racially mixed gathering, "The white blood harms us, it hurts us. When we was darker, we was stronger. We was purer."

of fancy. His vivid imagination was manifested before new acquaintances in his various claims of having been a sheikh, Hindu, or Mexican, and in grandiose moneymaking schemes that never panned out. There's little doubt that Ali's future volcanic monologues as an up-and-coming fighter were influenced by the father's wild, loquacious nature. As Ali would see it, "That's why I talk so much—cause he outtalks me!"

Clay, Sr., was also an inveterate womanizer whose ways, even in middle age, were not lost on Ali. "My father is a real hep-cat," Ali was quoted in *Sting Like a Bee,* a 1971 biography by José Torres. "Fifty-seven years old—crazy about the girls. He can't ride down the street without turning around. He outlooks me." Once while driving around Louisville, Clay, Sr., left young Cassius in the car while he himself jumped on a city bus, only to get off a block later. "I just wanted this girl's phone number," he explained to Cassius when he returned.

Louisville was still segregated in Cassius Clay's youth, much as it would remain when he returned to a hero's welcome from the Rome Olympics in 1960. The "separate but equal" world of "whites only" signs would leave a strong imprint on Cassius, who already as a young child was quick to recognize racial injustice. As an adult he would recall crying in bed at age ten over the unfairness of racism.

Perhaps the most shocking impression of all was the 1955 murder of Emmitt Till, a black youth from Chicago who had allegedly insulted a white woman in Mississippi. The fourteen-year-old boy was dragged at night from his relatives' home and drowned in the Tallahatchie River; three white men were arrested, tried, and found not guilty. The terrible crime and its aftermath was bitterly hashed over for weeks around the Clay household. "I couldn't get Emmitt out of my mind," Ali would say in *The Greatest,* while relating a story of how at the time he had vandalized a train yard as "a way to get back at white people for his death."

In *Muhammad Ali: His Life and Times*, by Thomas Hauser, Rahaman Ali (Ali's brother Rudy) matter-of-factly described Kentucky apartheid in the 1950s: "I never got into any fights. No one attacked me. It wasn't like the Deep South, but people would call us nigger and tell us to get out if they thought we were someplace we didn't belong."

It was the economic inequities of prejudice that weighed heavily on Cassius Clay, Sr., who would ramble long and loud about the white man as the devil who wound up with all the money. Little surprise that Ali, early in his career, would himself expound dreamily (and accurately, as it turned out) on a world of Cadillacs, great mansions, and the trappings of material wealth that lay just around the corner. That the best things in life weren't free and that whites should not be trusted were probably the two most common lessons regularly hammered home in the Clay household. It's ironic in this sense that the racial dogma preached by the father would play no small formative role in Muhammad Ali's ultimate embrace of the separatist tenets of the Nation of Islam—an act that Clay, Sr., himself could never reconcile.

If Ali would inherit considerable amounts of his father's fire and brimstone, so, too, could he thank his mother for her soft and gentle nature, for transmitting to the son a homespun, spiritual kindness. No one had been better to him his whole life, Ali always said, often referring to his mother as a "sweet little fat, homey mother . . . as sweet as she can be." As amazingly photogenic as Ali was, there lies, beneath the mock-angry ring poses, an almost courtly, gentle presence. Call it serenity and beauty as passed on by the mother, a soothing, light-skinned woman who was in every manner the direct opposite of her mate.

When Rudy was born two years after Cassius, the Clays purchased a four-room clapboard house for $4,500 at 3302 Grand Avenue, an elm-lined address in a quiet black neighborhood. The modest, boxlike abode had a small backyard; while hardly the lap of luxury, it was, nevertheless, light-years removed from Snake Town, Louisville's rugged downtown ghetto.

On Grand Avenue the Clay boys moved through their grammar school years in a modern-day, loosely urban Huck Finn fashion, replete with touch football, marbles (Cassius was a sharpshooter, unbeatable in the neighborhood), and lots of playing hooky. There was some running around with gangs, but it was mostly harmless stuff when compared with today's inner cities. Rock fights were common, and that, according to Ali, is where he learned to bob and weave as a boxer. "He used to ask me to throw rocks at him," said Rahaman Ali. "I thought he was crazy, but he'd stand back and dodge every one of them. No matter how many I threw, I could never hit him."

The older Cassius always protected his brother Rudy, who from an early age tagged along in his shadow. Even as a child, Cassius would save Rudy from a spanking, running in and grabbing his mother's arm. "Don't you hit my baby," he'd say. Physically, the two grew as opposites: the light-skinned Cassius resembling the mother in all her softness; the darker Rudy a spitting image of the chiseled-featured, mustachioed father. But the two boys would always remain close—as children in the playgrounds and later, in the boxing world of their adult lives, where Ali would one day shelter his fellow pugilist/brother from continuing a profession that posed serious threats to his health.

There's a tendency to assume that greatness was predestined in one form or another for Muhammad Ali, that boxing just happened along. Still, one can't help but look back and lay due importance on the seemingly innocuous event that set him careening toward crowning fame and glory.

⬦ ⬦ ⬦

"I'd mouth off to anybody who would listen . . ."

On a drizzly October day in 1954, twelve-year-old Cassius Clay was out riding bikes with his best friend, Johnny Willis. Looking for something different to do, they checked on a recreation center where an annual black merchandising show was going on. The lure here was free soda and hot dogs, and for Cassius, a chance to show off his brand-new Schwinn—a red, white, and chrome model with white sidewall tires.

The boys spent most of the afternoon at the show, stuffing themselves with candy and popcorn. Around seven, the place started to empty, and they decided to leave. When they got outside it was pouring rain, and it took Cassius a while to realize that his new bike had been stolen. When he did, he broke down in tears; the bike was a present that had cost $65, and he was afraid of his father's reaction. A passerby took notice and told the boys that there was a police officer running the boxing gym downstairs, that they ought to report the theft there.

"He was having a fit, half crying because someone stole his bike," the officer, Joe Martin, recalled on an HBO TV special. "He was gonna whup whoever stole it. And I brought up the subject, I said, 'Well, you better learn how to fight before you start challenging people that you're gonna whup.'"

Martin wrote up an official report on the stolen bike. Since he trained amateur boxers in his spare hours, five days a week,

Martin gave Cassius an application in case he wanted to join. The future champ had gotten his first look at boxing, and he liked what he saw. He would always remember the Columbia Gym and his first glimpse of boxing—sights, sounds, and smells that excited him so much that he almost forgot about the bike.

But the application was discarded when Cassius got home. As expected, he caught hell from his father, who was furious about the bike. Then about a week later, while watching a local television program called "Tomorrow's Champions," Cassius recognized Joe Martin in the ring with his fighters. The mere thought of the chance to appear on television appealed to a vanity that had already grown to colossal proportions. He asked his father's permission to sign up, and it was granted. A few days later, Cassius showed up at the gym and laced up the gloves at the first opportunity. The rest, as they say, is history.

As a twelve-year-old, ninety-five-pound string-bean novice, Cassius Clay was hardly an imposing figure inside the ropes at the Columbia Gym. On his first day, he unwisely jumped into the ring against an older fighter. Clay tried whaling away with wild, looping punches; before the round was over, his nose was bloodied, his head was reeling, and he had to be yanked to safety by another fighter. But he was hardly discouraged.

Cassius showed great speed and reflexes in his early days in the gym, but other than that, there wasn't any more or less promise to his amateur abilities than that of any of the thousands of boys Martin had already worked with. There was one attribute, however, that set him apart from all the rest back then, as it would always: determination. Once he'd acclimated himself to boxing's timeworn methods of training, no one could equal his single-mindedness of purpose.

"I realized it was almost impossible to discourage him," said Martin. "He was easily the hardest worker of any kid I've ever taught. Even then he was a little on the smart-alecky side, but he was a kid willing to make the sacrifices necessary to achieve something worthwhile in sports."

Six weeks after the stolen bike, Martin told Clay he was set for his first amateur bout and that it would be included in the next televised fight card. That propelled Cassius to canvass his neighborhood, to knock on doors and proclaim: "I'm Cassius Clay, and I'm having a fight on television. I hope you'll watch me." He would announce the date, time, and channel, and, not surprisingly, he would add that he was going to win.

Those who did tune in saw Clay defeat a white opponent named Ronnie O'Keefe in a three-round split decision—a wild, free-swinging brawl of a bout that had fans on their feet from the opening to the closing bell. From that day on, Clay, Sr., took to bragging to everyone who would listen that his son was a future champion. With the support of his proud parents—and later his teachers and the entire community—Cassius would fight an average of once every three weeks. It wasn't long before his colossal ego and cocksure arrogance were growing in direct proportion to his rapidly improving abilities.

"Almost from my first fights," Ali would tell José Torres, "I'd mouth off to anybody who would listen about what I was going to do to whoever I was going to fight. People would go out of their way to come and see, hoping I would get beat. When I was no more than a kid fighter, they would put me in bills because I was a drawing card, because I run my mouth so much. Other kids could battle and get all bloody and lose or win and didn't hardly nobody care. . . . But the minute I would come in sight, people would start hollering, 'Bash in his nose!' or 'Button his fat lip!' or something like that. I didn't care what they said as long as they kept coming to see me fight. They paid their money, they was entitled to a little fun. You would have thought I was some well-known pro, ten years older than I was."

Brashness aside, Cassius Clay, from his very first hours in the gym, devoted himself to becoming the best amateur boxer in the world. At school, his academic performance, never brilliant to begin with, would rapidly decline as he discovered the world of boxing. (He "graduated" 367th out of 391 in his class, receiving a "Certificate of Attendance" only because of his athletic achievement; he never learned to read adequately, a failing he would rue well into adulthood.) But in the boxing arena, he thirsted for knowledge. And he learned fast.

Clay was fascinated by every aspect of boxing. His teenage years were almost entirely dedicated to studying the fight game and to training. He shadowboxed incessantly in front of mirrors; he spent long hours jumping rope; he peppered the speed bag with quickly acquired coordination; he pounded the heavy bag with an intensity that belied his lithe body; and he sparred at every opportunity. He loved watching and talking with prizefighters, quizzing veteran trainers, and generally absorbing everything he could about gyms and boxing lore. This would become a true vocational love affair that would carry him long into his career.

"I started boxing and it was like God telling me that boxing was my responsibility," the retired Muhammad Ali told biographer Thomas Hauser. "Some people have special resources inside, and when God blesses you to have more than others, you have a responsibility to use it right."

For all aspiring fighters, a litmus test of training is the acceptance of the arduous roadwork necessary to build up stamina. From the moment he started working out, Cassius loved to run. Even as a thirteen-year-old, he was up daily at five in the morning, logging several miles before the sun was up. After that, he'd run alongside the bus and race it twenty-eight blocks to school, oblivious to the kids inside who laughed down at him. Sometimes he'd even footrace the thoroughbreds training at nearby Churchill Downs—that is, until the day he was barred for frightening a wild-eyed colt and nearly causing an accident. Cassius loved racehorses; their superb conditioning inspired his own quest for a perfect body.

And it wouldn't take long for Clay to begin developing the rudiments of his inimitable ring style. Most importantly, he relied on sheer speed. Without it, he'd have been a sitting duck, since he insisted on pulling or snapping his head straight back to avoid getting hit, rather than "slipping" punches by moving side to side—the heretofore infallible standard of boxing defense. Despite his disdain for the orthodox, he had superb instincts and movement. When ring veterans would warn him that he was bound to get clocked, he would smile and politely remind them that his method was similar to the lean-back style of Jack Johnson, the controversial heavyweight champion of a half century past (although technically, Clay's personal ring artistry was fashioned after that of his idol, Sugar Ray Robinson). And as Cassius grew rapidly in size and strength, his lightning-fast speed became all the more remarkable.

Setbacks occurred sporadically over his five-year amateur career, but Cassius was resilient. (Clay's amateur career record is a bone of contention: He and others have claimed anywhere from 160 to 190 bouts with 6, 7, or 8 losses; Joe Martin insisted there were exactly 106 fights with 6 losses, and that he, Martin, was present as trainer at every one of them.) There was a scary diagnosis of a heart murmur at age fifteen that forced him out of the ring for five months, but it proved to be a false alarm. Once, suffering from the flu, he dropped a decision to lifelong friend

With Joe Martin, the man who introduced young Cassius Clay to boxing.

Jimmy Ellis (who would briefly reign as heavyweight champ during Ali's exile). Another time, as Joe Martin recalled in *Black Is Best* by Jack Olsen, Clay was knocked out cold—the only time ever—while sparring with Willy Moran, a fellow amateur. "He really flattened Cassius that day," said Martin. "Cassius had been talking to me about wanting a scooter, and when he regained consciousness, he said, 'Which way was that scooter going that hit me?' It didn't faze him. He was back working with Moran the next day."

Cassius Clay nearly never made it to Rome. Following his frightful flight to the Olympic trials in California, he tore up his return plane ticket, borrowed train fare, and swore never to fly again. When he found out that it was too late to book a boat crossing to Europe, he insisted he would stay put rather than represent his country abroad. But when his trainer suggested to him that every Olympic win was worth $20,000 as a pro, that the gold-medal winner was assured of at least a top ten ranking, Cassius decided the gamble of one more flight was worth the risk.

And was it ever. Clay was an instant hit at the Olympic Village, where he thrived both as competitor and amateur diplomat. Displaying his snazzy, hands-low showboat style, he won over fans with the effortless ease of his preliminary wins over the Russian Schatkov and Tony Madigan, the Australian he'd beaten in Chicago. In the final, he jabbed and danced circles around rugged Pole Zbigniew Pietrzykowski (a veteran of more than 231 bouts) before overpowering him at the end. Outside the ring, he basked in the international limelight. "You would have thought he was running for mayor," said one of his team-mates. "He went around introducing himself and learning other people's names and swapping team lapel pins. If they'd had an election, he would've won it in a walk."

At a press conference, a Soviet reporter ("a Commie cat," according to Clay) asked the gold-medal winner how he felt about segregated restaurants back home. Refusing the bait, Clay answered with homespun swagger: "Tell your readers we've got qualified people working on that problem, and I'm not worried about the outcome. To me the U.S.A. is still the best country in the world, counting yours. It may be hard to get something to eat sometimes, but anyhow I ain't fighting alligators or living in a mud hut."

"This cat is a good one, Angie."

In 1956, Cassius Clay won his first title, a novice Golden Gloves title. By this time his ritual bragging made him easily the least popular fighter among his peers—a small price to pay for the pleasures gained from his indefatigable self-promotion. The following year, his future pro trainer Angelo Dundee brought light-heavyweight contender Willie Pastrano to Louisville for a fight. Cassius found their hotel and phoned their room. "This is Cassius Clay, the next heavyweight champion talking," he announced. "I'm gonna win the Olympics and be the next heavyweight champ. I'm in the lobby. Can I come up?"

Dundee invited him up, and for three hours Clay amused them by talking about himself and asking endless questions about training regimens, ring secrets, what to eat, etc. Decades later, Dundee would still shake his head over the audacity of the fifteen-year-old amateur fighter. When future champ Pastrano was again in town two years later, sparring was arranged with Cassius. After but one round, Pastrano appeared slow and helpless against Clay's speed. "What's the matter with you?" Dundee asked his fighter. "Hey, it ain't me," said Pastrano, shaking his head. "This cat is a good one, Angie."

In 1958, Clay, now 6 feet, 1 inch and 170 pounds and still growing, won the Louisville Golden Gloves before losing an impressive semifinal in the nationals in Chicago. The next year he followed the same path, but this time he won the national title by soundly thrashing a veteran Australian twelve years his senior. A few months later, after winning the AAU light-heavyweight title, he missed a chance for the Pan American Games when he dropped a close decision in the trials to a talented southpaw, a Marine named Amos Johnson. Warmly congratulating the winner, Clay accepted the loss stoically, saying that he hadn't been able to figure out his opponent. It would be thirteen years before he would lose another fight.

By 1960, the house on Grand Avenue was crowded with trophies and plaques as Clay had become a polished amateur champion, full of confidence and flash. His dazzling footwork and hand speed, his rapid-fire combinations, made dancing bears of even the most talented of his opponents. This would be his most active year in the amateurs, one during which he approached his craft with a consummately professional attitude. Again, he won the national Golden Gloves, this time entered as a heavyweight, so as not to encounter his light-heavyweight brother Rudy, who'd competed in local preliminaries. In the finals in Madison Square Garden Cassius was losing on points when he unleashed a furious rally to knock out an opponent who outweighed him by forty pounds. "Let's forget the Olympics," he told Joe Martin at the time. "I'm ready to turn pro."

Before Cassius Clay could conquer the world, he would have to overcome a near-paralytic fear of flying. After U.S. boxing officials pleaded with him to compete in the Olympic trials in San Francisco, he reluctantly booked a flight and nearly fainted when the plane hit a thunderstorm en route. Shaken by the trip, he nonetheless cruised through the trials, save for an alarming knockdown by one Allen Hudson, his opponent in the finals. Clay easily beat the count, and after winking at his trainer, he tore into his adversary and dis-

The Clay family: brother Rudy, left, Cassius, Jr., mother Odessa, and father Cassius, Sr.

patched him with a flurry of combinations. As Martin would acknowledge some years later, "Cassius really knew how to fight when he was in trouble." Martin was talking about the courage of a young amateur champion. But how could he, or anyone else, for that matter, even begin to imagine the amount of heart the future champion would have to call on—both in and outside the ring?

May 1963

CHAPTER TWO

EARLY ROUNDS

Relishing his newfound celebrity, Cassius Clay returned from Rome every bit the conquering hero. Cheering crowds, a ticker-tape parade, and a key to the city awaited him in Louisville. The porch steps of the house on Grand Avenue were painted red, white, and blue, and Clay's father sang "God Bless America" as his son pulled up to the curb with a police escort.

On his trip home, Clay had stopped over in New York City, where he stayed at the Waldorf-Astoria, courtesy of William Reynolds, a Louisville aluminum heir bent on handling his professional career. Wearing his U.S.A. blue blazer, his Olympic gold medal draped around his neck—he hadn't taken it off since the medal ceremony—Cassius strolled the city streets beaming at the dozens of people who recognized him. ("I guess everybody do know who I am," he told an accompanying reporter.) He stopped at a Times Square penny arcade and had a wishful headline made up: CASSIUS SIGNS FOR PATTERSON FIGHT ("back home, they'll think it's real"). And at the hotel, he wolfed five steaks a day from room service.

Reynolds made a big play for Clay's services. He had the medal winner brought to a Fifth Avenue jeweler to select expensive watches for Clay's parents. He offered Clay a $10,000 signing bonus, along with a ten-year guaranteed annual income. He flew Joe Martin (who, because of illness in his family, hadn't traveled to Rome) to New York, with the assumption that he would continue to train Cassius.

But Clay wasn't entirely comfortable with the Reynolds offer. For one thing, the fighter had over the past year begun to distance himself from Martin, preferring instead the technical assistance of a black trainer named Fred Stoner. For another, there was the unsettling experience of a pre-Olympics summer job Reynolds had provided that entailed Clay's cleaning toilets and generally being treated like a houseboy. Also, there was a flood of other proposals on the table, since Clay was now a very hot commodity. And finally, not to be overlooked was the influence of Clay, Sr.; the father had a deep mistrust of cops and resented Martin for receiving what he perceived as too much credit for his son's success.

So Clay rejected Reynolds and Martin, opting instead to sign with a Louisville group of eleven men, headed by an ex-actor named William Faversham. The deal was a good one for a fledgling pro: $10,000 up front, $40,000 over two years, liberal training expenses, and 50 percent of future purse monies. Clay immediately bought a 1959 pink Cadillac, and gave the remainder of the bonus to his parents for home renovations. As for Martin, the man who'd introduced him to boxing and had guided him to every one of his hundred-plus amateur wins was out. The fight game is not a place for sentiment. With designs on a title belt, Clay felt that Martin was too much of an amateur trainer. "I need top-notch people," Clay explained.

On October 29, a mere two months after the Olympics, Clay was back in the ring for his professional debut. Amid great anticipation, the fight, held in Louisville's Freedom Hall before some six thousand fans, turned out a bit of a dud—an uninspired six-round decision over Tunney Hunsaker, a police chief from Fayetteville, West Virginia. In the third round, Clay had pummeled his opponent to the brink but couldn't seem to finish him off. Still, Hunsaker, a pro veteran of twenty-five fights, would tell a colleague the next day that he was certain he had just lost to the future heavyweight champion.

Despite Clay's faith in Fred Stoner, who worked his corner for that first bout, the prefight training atmosphere was less than top-notch. In effect, Clay trained himself, telling friends, "He's [Hunsaker] a bum. I'll lick him easy." Without proper protection (untaped hands, no headguards), he sparred sporadically with his brother Rudy on a concrete basement floor. Just hours before the fight, Cassius ill-advisedly devoured a couple of steaks, which against a better body puncher could have cost him dearly. Clearly he needed some serious guidance to progress to championship levels. Since Clay's top training choices, Sugar Ray Robinson and Joe Louis, had already turned him down—both considered him overrated—the sponsors decided to send Clay out West to work with the legendary Archie Moore.

Archie Moore's spartan training digs were situated in an old salt mine in the hills outside San Diego. A character and master talker in his own right (and a veteran of more than two hundred fights), Moore was nonetheless a strict disciplinarian, rigidly set in his ways about developing a fighter. During his stay, the fiercely independent Cassius showed little patience for requi-

THE LOUISVILLE GROUP

The eleven-member Louisville sponsorship group was founded by investment counselor William Faversham for the express purpose of managing Cassius Clay. The idea was to gather a distinguished group of investors, a management team that would offer Clay the security to develop professionally, in exchange for a share of future profits. Ranging in age from twenty-five to seventy-five, Faversham's recruits were all white, all affluent, and most all of them were linked to Kentucky's whiskey, newspaper, Thoroughbred, and tobacco aristocracy. Members included Worth Bingham, whose family then owned Louisville's two newspapers as well as the CBS-TV affiliate; William Lee Lyons Brown, who was then chairman of the board of Brown-Forman, the distillery responsible for Old Forester, Jack Daniel's, and Early Times; and William Sol Cutchins, who was president of Brown and Williamson Tobacco Corporation.

For an untested fighter, the money—the bonus, guarantees, and expenses—wasn't bad. For the investors, each of whom put up $2,800, the deal wasn't too shabby, either—not when considering the publicity for themselves and their companies, the excitement, and the returns yet to come. With his rapidly growing black consciousness, Clay could hardly have been thrilled with depictions at the time of how these patrician gents were so charitably looking after the po'boy's future.

Surely, a few of the well-heeled members were altruistic in their motivation. Boxing, then as now, was a sewer, and here was a "clean" chance to steer one of Louisville's own clear from exploitation. But others in the group could just as surely use the scratch. As one "anonymous" investor was quoted in *Sports Illustrated* at the time: "Let me give you the official line—we are behind Cassius Clay to improve the breed of boxing, to do something for a deserving, well-behaved Louisville boy and finally, to save him from the jaws of the hoodlum jackals. . . . I think it's 50 percent true but also 50 percent hokum. What I want to do, like a few others, is to make a bundle of money."

Cassius Clay's contract with the Louisville sponsorship group expired in 1967. Rather than renewing the agreement, Ali turned to Herbert Muhammad to act as his manager, a job which Muhammad performed for the balance of Ali's career.

site menial tasks such as dishwashing and mopping floors and little respect for the instructor who tried to change his style. Clay also didn't take kindly to Moore's refusal to spar with him. "The boy needed a good spanking," Moore would say decades later, "but I wasn't sure who could give it to him." Clay lasted six weeks before he was on a train headed back to Louisville.

❖   ❖   ❖

"The boy needed a good spanking . . ."

Meanwhile, Bill Faversham had spoken with Miami-based trainer Angelo Dundee about his possibly handling Clay. Dundee, experienced and streetwise beyond his years, was an excellent choice for the "hands off" guidance necessary to deal with such a prodigious talent. Dundee was willing, but said it would have to wait until after Christmas. Clay couldn't wait, insisting he had to box—the sooner the better. The easygoing trainer relented, and within days he was greeting Clay at the Miami train station. From the start, they were a perfect match and would remain so during the two tumultuous decades to follow. As Dundee once said regarding his prize pupil, "The whole thing was to understand him."

Dundee immediately recognized Clay's special skills; it was merely left for him to polish them. "This is a new kind of person," Dundee would inform boxing scribes, "this is a special case where you can't give orders. He doesn't like being yelled at when he works out." What Dundee couldn't have foreseen was how much his new charge loved to work out. From his shared room in a run-down hotel, Clay would walk five miles to Dundee's Fifth Street Gym in Miami, train for hours, then plead to take on all comers in the ring. "This is my easiest job," said Angelo. "The guy's a glutton for work."

Another factor that eased Dundee's work was Clay's diffidence toward the fairer sex. He liked "foxes," as he called them (and treated them royally), but he was very green regarding romance. (Years after the Olympics, he revealed that he'd had a secret crush on sprint champion Wilma Rudolph, yet was too shy to approach her.) He also held to the old boxing credo that training and women don't mix. So, as a late teen, Clay's love life was virtually nonexistent—a situation that would one day dramatically reverse itself.

Dundee still had his work cut out, especially considering the need to gradually add professional touches that would make his fighter a more complete boxer. (Rather than gamble on 10 percent of purses, Dundee initially signed on for $125 a week—an indication of his caution.) Most famously, Dundee taught Clay how to "shoot" the jab; but there remained much-needed work on infighting, body punching, power punching, and all the assorted subtleties and various tricks that make up "the sweet science." Perhaps most important of all was keeping the fighter mentally tuned.

Pressing hard for an immediate fight, Clay was granted a date just before New Year's. That second pro appearance, against a local Miami knockabout named Herb Siler, wasn't much more impressive than the first, considering the opposition. Still, Clay did manage a fourth-round knockout—a right to the belly and a left hook to the jaw. After the pushover, he screamed, "I'm gonna beat Floyd Patterson, I'm gonna be heavyweight champ!" At the time, people just laughed.

Although Clay had enjoyed the high visibility of Olympic success a few months earlier, his early pro fights—aside from his hometown debut—hardly gleaned any press attention at all. Until a pro fighter has accumulated a truly impressive ring record against quality opponents, his championship potential is rarely even mentioned, much less considered. As far as the press, and in turn, the public were concerned, Clay was at this point simply a good-looking heavyweight with the gift of gab.

But what Clay did have going for him, besides talent, was a limitless capacity for self-promotion; if he barked loud enough, he'd get attention. Invited to spar a few rounds with former champ Ingemar Johansson, who was training for a rematch with Floyd Patterson, Clay crashed the Swede's camp, hollering, "I'll go dancin' with Johansson!" Try as he might, the number-one-ranked heavyweight couldn't lay a glove on Clay, who flitted around the ring, peppering him with jabs—all the time insisting that he himself should be fighting Patterson. "What does this kid do?" snarled Johansson after his trainer quickly called a halt. "Ride a bicycle ten miles a day?" The story made the news wires as the squeaky wheel got the oil.

But Clay didn't just want to be champion, he also wanted to be the youngest heavyweight champ in history. "This is an age of records," he explained then. "If you don't break some records, you're a no one." Wasting precious little time, he began 1961 with three wins over a five-week period. On his nineteenth birthday he scored a third-round TKO; three weeks later, a dazzling first-round knockout. His fifth, and most impressive victory thus far, came at the expense of Donnie Fleeman, a veteran fighter of forty-five wins—one of them a KO of former champ Ezzard Charles. Savvy enough to deflect Clay's combinations yet unable to handle his speed, Fleeman was stopped on cuts over the eyes in the seventh.

Next, Clay traveled back to Louisville to meet the first of the many dangerous sluggers he would face over his long career. That encounter, with Utah farmer Lamar Clark, was significant in that, (1) Clay withstood Clark's best punch—a staggering right to the jaw, the sort of blow that had gained the visitor forty-five straight knockouts, (2) Clay displayed his own power with three knockdowns in the second round, the last a lights-out closer, and (3) Clay predicted the round in which he would win.

"I said he would fall in two," said Clay, who'd been introduced as the "Louisville Larruper," and he did. "I'll continue this approach to prove I'm great. From now on they all must fall in the round I call."

If Clay forgot to "call" his next couple of fights it was just as well, as both ended in ten-round decisions. In Las Vegas he dominated Duke Sabedong, an awkward giant from Hawaii; back in Louisville he won nine of ten rounds to outpoint Alonzo Johnson, once a sixth-ranked heavyweight. "Am I scared of getting beat by Johnson?" Clay had asked rhetorically before the fight. "If a man intends to buy a Lincoln Continental next month, does he worry about the cost of a Ford to get him around in the meantime? Floyd Patterson is the Continental and Johnson is the Ford that will help me drive down to the showroom."

The Sabedong fight would best be remembered for Clay's fortuitous encounter with wrestler Gorgeous George; the Johnson fight for being Clay's pro debut on national television (Gillette's Friday night fights). Recalling the latter, Dundee said, "He boxed smart and was able to connect with clean punches. I thought he was ready for the big leagues."

On the day before his ninth pro fight, Cassius Clay let the world know that he had just shaved for the first time ever and that his opponent, Alex Miteff, would "fall in six." But Clay almost blew the forecast when he began hammering the beefy Argentinian in the first—an impulse to impress those critics

◆ GORGEOUS GEORGE ◆

GORGEOUS GEORGE WITH HIS NUMBER-ONE FAN.

Cassius Clay was plugging his fight with Duke Sabedong on a radio talk show in Las Vegas when he met fellow guest Gorgeous George Wagner, the eminent wrestler of the day. In comparatively subdued fashion, Cassius told listeners how he was going to win, how it was going to be a tough fight, etc. When it came Gorgeous George's turn (he was also appearing in the same arena), he grabbed the mike and began screaming about how he was going to annihilate his opponent, how he would cut all his own long hair off if he lost—but that it would never happen since he was "the greatest wrestler in the world."

Clay, who knew a few things about mouthing off, decided to go watch George in action. He was amazed as the wrestler, hair in curlers, entered the ring with a personal attendant to comb out his long golden locks, to spray him with a perfume atomizer, and to tend to his sequined robe. As Gorgeous George then proceeded to brutalize some hapless foil, the crowd howled with disapproval. Clay loved the act and tore out a few pages for his own book.

"I saw fifteen thousand people coming to see this man get beat," Clay would recall, "and his talking did it. I thought this was a good idea." Backstage, Wagner advised Clay: "A lot of people will pay to see someone shut your mouth. So keep on bragging, keep on sassing, and always be outrageous." It was no doubt Wagner's influence that resulted in one of Clay's most familiar refrains: "Look at me, I'm so pretty."

who claimed he "hopped around" too much. Failing an immediate knockout, Clay chose to box over the ensuing rounds,
and the fight turned relatively close. Midway through the sixth,
however, Clay unloaded a crunching right—for years he rated
it his best punch ever thrown—that collapsed Miteff to the
canvas on schedule.

Clay targeted his next opponent, Willie Besmanoff, for the
seventh round, adding that he was "embarrassed to get in the
ring with this unrated duck." The slur infuriated his German
foe, who rushed Clay at the opening bell, albeit unsuccess-
fully. While Dundee repeatedly implored him to "stop playing
around," Clay blithely bided his time until round seven, when
his series of rapid-fire combinations brought matters to a
quick close.

"I'm the onliest one."

By this time, one year into his career, Clay's bold pronouncements had captured the public eye. Sportswriters
inured to pulling teeth for quotes from athletes had never been
exposed to the likes of such voluble braggadocio. And it was-
n't just the predictions; it also was the totality of Clay's sense
of importance—the sheer freethinking, free-associative manner in which he expressed himself.

On heaven and hell: "When I've got me a $100,000 house,
another quarter million stuck in the bank, and the world title
latched onto my name, then I'll be in heaven. Walking around
making $25 a week, with four children crying at home 'cause
they're hungry, that's my idea of hell. I ain't studying about
either one of them catching up with me in the graveyard."

On his skills: "I got the height, the reach, the weight, the physique, the speed, the courage, the stamina, and the natural ability . . . to beat me, you got to be greater than great."

On his meteoric rise: "All the time someone is telling me, 'Cassius, you know I'm the one who made you.' . . . Listen here: When you want to talk about who made me, you talk to me. Who made me is me."

On himself: "I'm the onliest one."

New York City's Madison Square Garden was a natural venue for a natural showman. The historic arena beckoned with a bout against Sonny Banks, a banger from Detroit whom Clay decided would "fall in four." But Banks almost spoiled that agenda with a lurching left hook in the first that sent Cassius to the canvas for the first time as a pro—much to the delight of fans who'd been eagerly anticipating just such a moment. Dundee turned white with alarm, but Clay, more surprised than hurt, was up at the count of two, cautiously boxing his way out of trouble. The rest was one-sided, as Clay, on cue, finished Banks in the fourth. Dundee would recall his fighter's first-round rebound as the moment when he "really fell in love with Clay."

Clay cruised through 1962 by winning six more fights, all by knockout, and all but one called correctly. After a fourth-round KO of Don Warner—previously "set" for the fifth—Clay explained he had decided to subtract a round when his opponent refused to shake hands at the opening bell. In July, he was motivated to dispatch Alejandro Lavorante in five, knowing that Archie Moore had taken ten rounds to do so a few months earlier. "What an old man can do, a young man can do better," said Clay. The stage was now set for an upcoming test against the old man who had so briefly tried to tame Clay two years past.

As probably the two most vocal fighters boxing has ever known, Clay and Moore ceaselessly bantered back and forth in the weeks leading up to their November 1962 bout. With gusts of nonstop hot air, Clay acted as if desperate to win what Moore called a "tournament of words." "Never send a boy on a man's errand," Moore proclaimed in a televised "debate." Clay answered him with a boastful rhyme:

> Archie's been living off the fat of the land—
> I'm here to give him his pension plan.
> When you come to the fight don't block the door,
> Cause you'll all go home after round four.

When Clay threatened to retire him with a "pension punch," Moore warned that he himself had a new weapon, a "Lip-buttoner." But boxing is a young man's game. Less than half Moore's age, Clay physically took charge inside the ring, with all the bounce and gusto he'd verbally commanded outside it. From the outset he controlled the action, and after two brutal knockdowns in the promised fourth, the fight was mercifully stopped.

The victory over Moore elevated Clay to fourth in the heavyweight rankings. In the meantime, Sonny Liston, only two months earlier, had obliterated Floyd Patterson in one round to become the new heavyweight champion. Replacing Patterson's name, Liston's was the one now repeatedly cross-ing Clay's lips, although boxing experts near-unanimously felt that the formidably lethal new champion was well out of the brash contender's league—at least for now. The two met in a Los Angeles ballroom after the Moore fight, whereupon Clay began baiting the champ in earnest: "Liston in eight! Liston in eight!" he ranted. "If you last more than eight seconds, you can have the fight," growled Liston, adding, "You couldn't lick a Popsicle."

A week after his twenty-first birthday, Clay scored again when he battered Charlie Powell, an ex-pro football player, into a predicted third-round submission. ("Beauty Beats Beast" had been Clay's suggested headline to newsmen before the fight.) It was his seventeenth win and seventh correct prognostication out of his last eight fights.

It's hard to tell how intoxicated Clay was with his own success at this point, since so much of his posturing was admittedly an act. Yet however much an act, the very ability to choreograph bouts against menacing top heavyweights was by itself fairly remarkable, if not an actual measure of pure championship talent. His pro record—carefully crafted by Dundee—had by now so built on itself, so infused him with self-confidence, that his aims on Liston's belt were anything but bluff. Dundee and the sponsorship group were still in no hurry, as a premature loss in a championship fight could ruin even the brightest career. But there was a question at some point as to how long Clay could be held back. He had become progressively forceful as a young adult, a man with very strong opinions of what the future held in store. Perhaps it was an eye on Liston that caused him to stumble in his eighteenth bout.

❧ ❧ ❧

"Why don't they boo for me?"

Even with a publicity-crippling newspaper strike, Clay managed to sell out Madison Square Garden for his March

❖ VINTAGE POETRY ❖

Call them poems, stanzas, couplets, rhymes, doggerel—whatever, Cassius Clay was surely the first athlete to so gloriously celebrate himself. A few samples from the early years:

❖

At the Louisville airport, upon returning from Rome:

> To make America the greatest is my goal,
> So I beat the Russian, and I beat the Pole,
> And for the U.S.A. won the medal of gold.
> Italians said, "You're greater than the Cassius of old.
> We like your name, we like your game,
> So make Rome your home if you will.
> I said I appreciate your kind hospitality,
> But the U.S.A. is my country still,
> 'Cause they waiting to welcome me in Louisville.

❖

On television, before the Archie Moore fight:

> It all started twenty years past
> The greatest of them all was born at last
> The very first word from his Louisville Lips,
> "I'm pretty as a picture, and there's no one I can't whip."
> Then he said in a voice that sounded rough,
> "I'm strong as an ox and twice as tough."
> The name of this champ, I might as well say—
> No other than the greatest, Cassius Clay.
> He predicts the round in which he's gonna win
> And that's the way his career has been.
> He knocks them all in the round he'll call,
> And that's why he's called the greatest of them all.

As part of prefight buildup, Clay's vision of the eighth round vs. Liston, "exactly as it will happen":

Clay comes out to meet Liston
And Liston starts to retreat
If Liston goes back any further
He'll end up in a ringside seat
Clay swings with a left
Clay swings with a right
Look at young Cassius
Carry the fight.
Liston keeps backing
But there's not enough room
It's a matter of time
There, Clay lowers the boom.
Now Clay swings with a right
What a beautiful swing
And the punch raises the bear
Clear out of the ring.
Liston is still rising
And the ref wears a frown
For he can't start counting
Till Sonny comes down.
Now Liston disappears from view
The crowd is getting frantic
But our radar stations have picked him up
He's somewhere over the Atlantic.
Who would have thought
When they came to the fight
That they'd witness the launching
Of a human satellite.
Yes, the crowd did not dream
When they lay down their money
That they would see
A total eclipse of the Sonny.
I am the greatest!

meeting with third-ranked Doug Jones. In a feverish promotional blitz he appeared on TV shows, stopped by nightclubs, shook hands on street corners, even spouted rhymes at a Greenwich Village coffeehouse ("This boy likes to mix, so I'll take him in six")—all to put the proverbial butts in the seats. The quiet Jones had little to say other than a mild vow that he'd "make Clay eat his words." But the last word, as usual, was Clay's: "I talk very good. I fight even better. And I pack 'em in."

Around this time, Clay met Drew Bundini Brown, a professional sidekick, world traveler, and former member of Sugar Ray Robinson's entourage. In Bundini, Cassius found a wild man, street poet, and personal cheerleader who loved to talk as much as he did. Brown was taken in and would rapidly become the de facto head of Clay's budding entourage. Their stormy, off-on relationship would last the better part of two decades.

Sixteen thousand fight fans packed the Garden, most hoping to see Clay lose. But he won again, barely, in a resourceful struggle—the decision of which brought a cascade of boos rippling all the way down from the cheap seats to ringside. For the first time in Clay's career, a well-schooled opponent had responded in kind with connecting jabs, timely combinations, and bothersome speed. In the ballyhooed sixth, fans jeered as the seconds ticked down on Clay's self-imposed deadline. But even if Clay was off, he stormed back in the middle rounds, and by the end was landing punches in bunches. The critics harrumphed loudly, the fans screamed "Fix!" but Dundee was pleased— his fighter had been seriously tested and had survived.

Afterward, in the dressing room, Clay was disconsolate. "Why did these people boo me when I whup him?" he asked *New Yorker* boxing scribe A. J. Liebling. "Why don't they boo for me?" With his 30 percent take of a sold-out house, Clay had profited well from the lessons of Gorgeous George. The fans had paid either to see him lose or work his called-round wizardry, and he had in a sense failed them—never mind the win. Still, he would grace the cover of *Time* the following week.

The relative difficulty of the Jones fight suggested that another tune-up was in order before taking on Liston. Thus did the Clay camp decide to take the act overseas against Henry Cooper, the slow yet highly rated British champ. As with his previous fight, Clay looked to Liston ("I'm only here to mark time before I annihilate that big, ugly bear") while training; and, as was getting to be a habit, he casually disrespected his opponent (and this time, an entire country); and, once again, he was lucky to escape a loss that might have ultimately cost him his title shot.

"After five rounds Henry Cooper will think his name is Gordon Cooper [the astronaut]," Clay told British newsmen. "He'll be in orbit." He predicted a fifth-round knockout. To further irk the populace, Clay called Buckingham Palace a "swell pad" and had the temerity to enter the ring at Wembley Stadium wearing a jeweled crown saying that he was the king. As Clay arrogantly held five fingers up to signify his KO round, fifty-five thousand fans screamed for his head. They almost got it.

By the fourth round Clay was in full command, taunting and jabbing Cooper, who was bleeding from cuts around both eyes. Then suddenly near the end of the round, a wild, sweeping left hook dumped Cassius to the canvas just before the bell. As Clay sat on his stool obviously dazed, Dundee shrewdly pulled open a small tear he'd noticed earlier on one of Clay's gloves and called the referee over to show him the damage. A new glove was fruitlessly sought, allowing Clay a precious extra minute to clear his head. Properly recuperated, he came out in

❖ ANGELO DUNDEE ❖

It's no big schmear, the job I do," Angelo Dundee once told reporters in his typically self-deprecating vein. "I lead a very uneventful life. I'm an ordinary guy."

It took just such an ordinary guy to hit it off with such an extraordinary guy as his employer: Cassius Clay. Theirs was a perfect marriage: the trainer who adapts to everyone, who treats no two fighters the same, matched with the most individualistic athlete sport has ever known, a boxer who would grudgingly listen to but one man in his entire spectacular ring career. But Dundee knew the deal, as well as how to deal. "Gee, your uppercut was working to perfection," he would tell Clay after a workout. Clay hadn't thrown an uppercut, but the next day he would.

Part psychologist, part fight strategist, and part old-fashioned Q-Tips-behind-the-ears cornerman, Dundee was a character in his own

ANGELO DUNDEE READIES ALI FOR SPARRING PRACTICE.

right, yet at the same time a calming presence in the turbulent world that would surround his greatest fighter. "If I was a person that got bugged, I'd be in an insane asylum," he said. "I love fighters."

Dundee's prime role as Ali's trainer and the trust Ali placed in him also worked to protect Dundee from that same turbulent world. Often the only Caucasian among Ali's entourage during a period of heightened racial tension, Dundee developed a friendship with Ali that transcended black and white.

"I like him 'cause he's half-colored," Clay once joked to José Torres. "He's Italian and he passes for white, but he's got a lot of nigger in him."

Not really, although Dundee was a swarthy Calabrese whose ethnic darkness Clay liked to joke about. Born and raised in Philadelphia, Dundee followed his brother Chris to New York City in the early fifties, hoping to learn the fight game. Chris Dundee was a well-known fight manager/promoter, and Angelo was content back then to start at the bottom, which meant carrying a water bucket. "There's a right way and wrong way of carrying a water bucket," he would one day recall. "I made a lot of mistakes. I spilled the bucket." Dundee carried most of his buckets while working at Stillman's Gym in New York, where he met such legendary trainers as Chickie Ferrera, Charley Goldman, and Ray Arcel. Much that Dundee brought to Ali's corner was learned at their side.

Eventually Angelo followed his brother to Miami to the famous Fifth Street Gym; his permanent residence there had a lot to do with its ultimate legendary status. Angelo's other renowned fighters over the years have included Luis Rodriguez, Carmen Basilio, and Willie Pastrano. But his most famous fighter after his years with Ali was Sugar Ray Leonard, gold-medal winner in the 1976 Olympics. Many saw similarities between Leonard and Ali; both were fast, if not exceptionally powerful, and both used the media to their great advantage. Dundee's presence in Leonard's corner seemed the final touch, and the between-rounds advice he gave to Leonard in Duran-Leonard I that spurred Sugar Ray on to a victory bore a memorable resemblance to his heroics on Ali's behalf in Ali-Liston I. Unfortunately for Leonard, the partnership lasted only a few years, finally ending over financial differences.

At the end of the day, Muhammad Ali was Dundee's brightest superstar. Many say that there will never be another Muhammad Ali.

But there will never be another Angelo Dundee, either.

With Henry Cooper, after Ali-Cooper I, 1963.

the fifth with a furious attack on the sliced-up Englishman,
and the fight was legitimately stopped one minute later.

For once, Clay was momentarily humble afterward in his
dressing room, calling Cooper the hardest puncher he'd faced

and expressing regret for having called him a bum. However, once he spotted Sonny Liston's manager, Jack Nilon, he lit up, telling him, "I'll demolish Sonny in eight, and he'll be in a worser fix if I predict six."

Standing nearby was Madison Square Garden matchmaker Teddy Brenner. "I hate to say it," he said, shaking his head, "but maybe the best thing that could happen to him would be to get a licking." That's what Archie Moore had thought as well, even as he bemoaned a lack of prospects for the job. But now it was evident that ex-convict Liston, hardly a popular champion, was just the man to silence the mouth that roared.

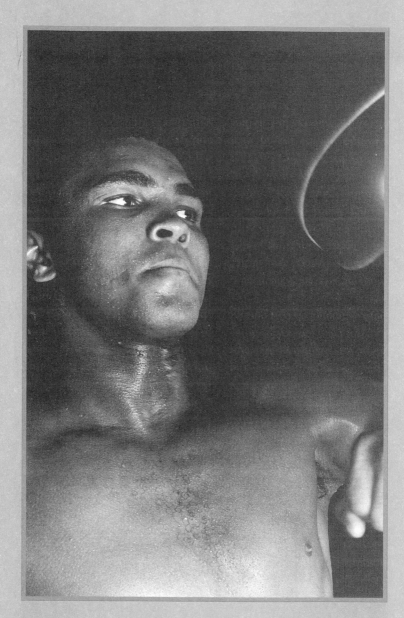

circa 1963

CHAPTER THREE

THE CHAMPION

Although Cassius Clay had been banging the drum loudly in his quest for a title shot with Sonny Liston, the bout was by no means imminent in the early summer of '63. Clay's people still thought the bout was premature, that their fighter wasn't yet "ready." Their feelings were reinforced after the Jones and Cooper fights exposed Clay's alleged defensive lapses. There were offers to square off against such valid contenders as Eddie Machen, George Chuvalo, and Ingmar Johansson, but Cassius himself nixed them all—he seemed obsessed with the crown.

For his part, Liston seemed pretty much to ignore Clay—as difficult as that might be. The champion focused instead on his late-July rematch with Floyd Patterson, after which he would decide on who would be the next victim. Meanwhile, Clay, with his own well-defined agenda, mounted a brilliant campaign to goad Liston into the ultimate showdown. Along the way, he tap-danced at will on the champion's fragile psyche.

In July Clay showed up in Las Vegas expressly to harass Sonny. He hounded Liston at the champion's training exhibitions, yelling to observers, "Look at him, he's so slow—he's just a flat-footed bear" and "I don't know whether I'll beat him or cage him." One evening at the Thunderbird Casino, where the sullen Liston was dropping serious money, there was Clay dogging him again, snatching up his dice in midthrow and calling him a loser who "couldn't even shoot craps." And after Liston crushed Patterson two minutes into the first round—a carbon-copy repeat of their previous meeting—Clay was there to spoil the party. "The fight was a disgrace!" he shouted, grabbing the ring microphone. "Liston is a tramp. I'm the champ. I want the big bum just as soon as I can get him." And this time Liston yelled back: "You're next, bigmouth!"

One of the wildest of Clay's schemes involved an early-morning visit to Liston's new home in Denver. Having alerted TV and radio stations well in advance, Clay and his entourage rolled into Sonny's quiet, and very white, neighborhood in a bus that had "World's Most Colorful Fighter" painted across the top. They honked the horn, they screamed, "Oink, oink!" Someone even laid a bear trap in the front yard. The police were called, Liston bitterly cursed his nemesis, and Clay, quite satisfied, beat a hasty, giggly retreat. As Clay himself had once opined, "a wise man can act a fool, but a fool can't act the wise man."

In November 1963 all of Clay's machinations finally paid off as Liston signed to fight him in Miami the following February. "If I'm not asleep, this is a dream come true," said Clay. Some feared it a nightmare and weren't so thrilled. "We did not want this fight so soon," a member of the sponsorship group explained, "but Cassius insisted and we had to give in. After all, it's his career."

✦ ✦ ✦

"It's my time to howl."

Clay put on quite a show in the months leading up to the fight. His training quarters at the Fifth Street Gym were a festive happening compared to Liston's somber daily workouts across town. ("I don't know what I'm training for," Liston would say, while his seconds took turns throwing a twelve-pound medicine ball against his abdomen. "This kid ain't gonna last one round.") Commanding center stage as if he'd been born there, chattering away as he shadowboxed, Clay offered veteran boxing scribes fresh material every day. "I talk to reporters till their fingers are sore," he would say, well aware that few among the fight crowd gave him any chance. Almost to a man, they predicted he would lose badly.

"The loudmouth from Louisville is likely to have a lot of vainglorious boasts jammed down his throat by a hamlike fist belonging to Sonny Liston, the malefic destroyer who is champion of the world," wrote *The New York Times*'s Arthur Daley. "Only in this time of soap bubble promotion could anyone take Clay seriously when he steps in the ring," wrote Milton Gross of *The New York Post*. "Clay should see a good psychiatrist," said former champ Rocky Marciano. In California there was even a politician/boxing abolitionist who warned of a "dangerous mismatch that could result in grave injury to the young challenger." Forty-three of forty-six boxing writers polled thought Liston would win. And the eleven living former heavyweight champions unanimously felt Clay wasn't ready.

◆ SONNY LISTON ◆

"A prizefight is like a cowboy movie," Sonny Liston once said. "There has to be a good guy and a bad guy. People pays their money to see me lose. Only in my cowboy movie, the bad guy always wins."

Charles "Sonny" Liston was a loser most of his life, save for the year and a half he ruled the heavyweight roost. Last of an Arkansas sharecropper's twenty-five children, he left home at age thirteen and spent his teenage years cracking heads as a union goon in St. Louis. By the time he'd become a ranked pro, he'd been arrested some twenty times and served five years for armed robbery.

At signings and prefight intros, Liston was the unchallenged master of the icy stare, the menacing glower that signaled impending doom for opponents. Veteran fighters seemed to wilt under the glare. Floyd Patterson took great pains to avoid eye contact and still got knocked silly. Liston had one of the great left jabs in history; his considerable skills as

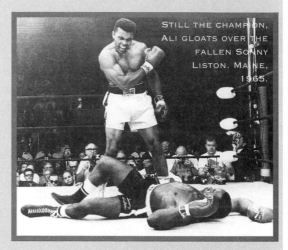

STILL THE CHAMPION, ALI GLOATS OVER THE FALLEN SONNY LISTON. MAINE, 1965.

a boxer were often overlooked, due largely to his awesome punching power.

It's a wonder that Liston ever became champion, what with his underworld management connections that were continually under investigation. His career was marked by extremes—on one end, the first-round KOs of Patterson; on the other, the controversial endings to his fights with Clay/Ali.

Sonny Liston died in relative obscurity in 1971 of a heroin overdose in his Las Vegas home. Foul play was suspected but was never proven. Said fight publicist Harold Conrad, summing up Liston's life: "I think he died the day he was born."

For Clay, the harshest indictment was that no one took him seriously. To cynical observers his image was that of a charlatan, a fraud, a money-hungry flash in the pan who had scored himself some publicity, a nice share of a big purse, and was due a rude awakening. Moreover, few believed that even he thought he could win. Clay was generally good-natured about his status, although at times he was clearly not amused.

"I'm keeping a list of all you people," he announced to onlookers at one of the final training sessions. "After the fight is done, we're going to have a roll call up there in the ring. And when I see so-and-so said this fight is a mismatch, why, I'm going to have a little ceremony and some eating is going on— some eating of words."

On the morning of the fight (February 25), the two parties gathered for the weigh-in—traditionally little more than a photo-op, since heavyweights have no upper limits on poundage. Clay used the occasion for one last prefight psychological confrontation with his adversary. Accompanied by his ever-growing entourage (led by Bundini Brown) and wearing a denim jacket with "bear hunting" scrawled on the back, Clay stomped into the Miami Convention Center screeching, "It's my time to howl," "rumble, man, rumble," and the now-classic "float like a butterfly, sting like a bee" (at times followed by "your hands can't hit what your eyes can't see")—a phrase that would eventually become synonymous with his dazzling ring style. Liston stood by impassively, perhaps even a bit dumfounded.

As Liston climbed the scales, Clay, eyes bulging, arms jerking wildly in the air, howled, "Chump! Chump!" He stood nose-to-nose with the champion—few realized that at 6 feet, 2½ inches, Clay was taller than Liston—his voice gone shrill: "I got you now, Sonny, I got your championship now." Clay made as if to lunge for the champ, whereupon a half dozen people struggled to restrain him, although Dundee would later say he was actually only holding him back with his pinkie. But when the Miami Boxing Commission doctor, Alexander Robbins, took Clay's blood pressure, the reading was a shocking 200/100—a sign of extreme hypertension that nearly caused cancellation of the fight (Robbins later surmised that Clay had whipped himself into a temporary frenzy). For his wild outburst, Clay was fined $2,500, a cheap price to pay for the psychological damage inflicted. "I don't think this kid's all there," grumbled Liston, the eight-to-one betting favorite. "I think he's scrambled in the marbles."

Which, as it turned out, was just what Clay wanted him to think. "Liston is a bully, and a bully is scared of a crazy man," Clay calmly told his personal physician, Ferdie Pacheco, as his blood pressure had returned to normal later that afternoon. "Now Liston thinks I'm crazy. I got him worried."

The action that night began predictably enough, with Liston trying his best to dislodge Clay's head. Clay, who would later admit just trying to survive that first round, did so with characteristic aplomb—flitting away from Liston's lethal haymakers while poking annoyingly with his own jab. The crowd gasped as the challenger landed a dazzling flurry of combinations on the snorting champ's face to end the round. In the third, Clay— now in control after six minutes of effective parrying—landed a nasty right that opened a deep gash on Liston's cheekbone. The blow wasn't so physically damaging as it was a humiliating reminder of the course the fight was taking. "At that moment," Clay would later say, "he looked like he's going to look twenty years from now."

The fourth round was relatively uneventful, but some caustic liniment got transferred from Liston's cut to his gloves and into Clay's eyes, temporarily blinding the challenger. "Cut the gloves off! I can't see!" Clay screamed to Dundee between rounds. "Leave me outta here."

"What are you talking about?" the trainer shot back. "This is for the big one, Daddy. This is for the title, and we aren't going to quit now." And with a shove in the rear, Dundee sent his reluctant charge out for the fifth, imploring him to "keep away" and box. Blinking continuously, Clay danced, backpedaled, and bobbed-and-weaved his way clear of the murderously aroused champion and managed to finish the round unscathed.

Clay's eyes had cleared by the sixth, a round in which he reestablished control with a vengeance. The crowd watched in amazement as the challenger battered the champion from all directions, lefts and rights slashing into Liston's squinting mug. Clay knew it was just a matter of time, but for Liston, the fight was already over. Blaming an injured shoulder, he spat out his mouthpiece and refused to answer the bell for the seventh.

Afterward, the ecstatic new champion spewed forth a torrent heard on radio broadcasts the world over: "I want everybody to bear witness. I am the greatest! I shook up the world! I don't have a mark on my face! I'm pretty! I'm a bad man! You must listen to me! I can't be beat! My face was burning and I whupped him! I'm the prettiest thing that ever lived! . . . I want justice."

Following his astounding victory, Clay's next-day press conference held an additional surprise, at least for the public at large. Speaking in a subdued voice, the new champion confirmed what insiders had known and what some columnists had been writing for the past few months: He was indeed a proud follower of Elijah Muhammad's Nation of Islam.

"I believe in Allah, and I believe in peace," answered Clay when asked by a reporter if he was a "card-carrying member of the Black Muslims." "I know where I'm going and I know the truth, and I don't have to be what you want me to be. I'm free to be what I want."

Let there be no mistake, Clay seemed to be saying—he would not be white America's lackey or even its role model in the manner of earlier popular heavyweight champions Joe Louis and Rocky Marciano. "Where do you think I'd be next week," asked Clay, "if I didn't know how to shout and holler and make the public take notice? I'd be poor and I'd probably be in my hometown, washing windows or running an elevator and saying 'yes, suh' and 'no, suh' and knowing my place. Instead of that, I'm one of the highest-paid athletes in the world. Think about that. A southern colored boy has made one million dollars."

These were provocative words coming from a star athlete, much less one who'd thus far been universally regarded as little more than a shallow showboat. Here was a champion black boxer publicly examining for the first time the political and social constricts of his world.

At a second press conference, Clay elaborated on his beliefs: "Black Muslims is a press word, not a legitimate name. . . . I ain't no Christian. I can't be when I see all the people for forced integration get blowed up. . . . I like white people. I like my own people. They can live together without infringing on each other. You can't condemn a man for want-ing peace. If you do, you condemn peace itself. A rooster crows only when it sees the light. Put him in the dark and he'll never crow. I have seen the light and I'm crowing."

Clay had first seen the light of Islam in 1961 when, after reading copies of *Muhammad Speaks*, the Nation's newspaper, he had attended a mosque meeting at the behest of a converted street hustler named Captain Sam. ("After that, my life changed," Ali would say years later.) As immersed as he was in his violent sport, Clay was at the same time deeply spiritual and well attuned to prevailing social injustice. With its upholding of black pride, its worship of a black God, and with its strict moral codes, the Nation of Islam presented an attractive package for a young black athlete seeking a righteous path. And at the mosque, Clay found comfort in the brotherhood, the cleanliness of spirit, the dietary laws, and the purity of women—all of which provided a certain protection for a dedicated boxer in serious training.

"After I beat him, I'll convert him."

Clay had practiced Islam for almost three years, quietly attending meetings through the back door, lest his new religion put his career in jeopardy. He'd also become a close friend and protégé of Malcolm X, who'd recently gained special notoriety for his public comment on the JFK assassination: "The chickens have come home to roost." Clay was well aware that his brethren were perceived as a "hate group" for their separatist tenets and their castigation of whites. In fact, just prior to the Liston fight, promoter Bill MacDonald had demanded that Clay publicly renounce the Muslims. Clay had refused, saying that if his faith was the reason for calling off the fight, then it should be called off. MacDonald, of course, relented; Malcolm, who'd been very much a visible part of the Clay contingent, helped cool matters by lying low until the postfight celebration, at which time he and the new champ ate vanilla ice cream together.

Even as Malcolm X had become a figurehead and spokesman for the Nation, a deep rift had grown between him and Elijah

Muhammad, a small, aging man who, for all his benign appearance, was a dogmatic leader. Malcolm formed a splinter group from his Harlem mosque, and followers took sides. Clay, now calling himself Cassius X (his "waiting name"), sided with Elijah, whose teachings, he claimed, had propelled him to victory. While Malcolm had in ways been Cassius X's Islamic mentor, Elijah, as Allah's messenger, was rapidly becoming a surrogate father figure to the new champion. Ironically, it was Malcolm who had told Clay before the Liston fight, "Do you think Allah has brought about all this intending for you to leave the ring as anything but champion?"

Within a month after defeating Liston, Cassius X became Muhammad Ali (meaning "worthy of all praise most high" in Arabic), the name given him by Elijah Muhammad. Participating in white man's sport, and particularly boxing, was anathema to Elijah, who would nevertheless forsake principle in exchange for the benefits of adding such a famous missionary to his cause.

Ali's Muslim affiliations did little for his public image; nor did they enhance his earning power outside the ring, as several proposed endorsement deals fell through. While he was briefly acclaimed in the press for his climactic title bid, most columnists were quick to turn on him for his religious beliefs, which years later they would grudgingly recognize to be legitimate. Ex-champion Jack Dempsey echoed popular sentiment when, while receiving a "sportsmanship" citation from House Speaker John McCormack, he attacked Clay for his religious stance and expressed doubts over whether the new champion was a "real American."

Public figures jumped on the anti-Clay/Ali bandwagon. Joe Louis avowed that "Clay will earn the public's hatred for his connections." Floyd Patterson, who had supposedly retired from boxing, swore to "win back the title for America." Martin Luther King called him "a champion of racial segregation." Even Ali's father felt that his son had been "conned" by the Muslims. Yet it seemed the more he was attacked, the stronger Ali held to his beliefs. "After I beat him, I'll convert him," he said of Patterson. As for Louis, Ali branded him a "sucker" for his well-publicized losing battles with the IRS.

Scarcely weeks after he'd become champ, Muhammad Ali began his own long struggle with the federal government. It all started with news released by Ali's draft board that he was unfit for service, based on his failing the intelligence test given to prospective inductees. This unleashed a nationwide furor as senators and congressmen received piles of letters from citizens wanting to know how a heavyweight champion could spout clever poetry yet still be considered too dumb to tote a rifle for Uncle Sam. Army psychiatrists insisted the test results were on the level, but people were skeptical. As Ali told *Playboy*, "I said I am the greatest. Ain't nobody ever heard me say I was the smartest."

Given Ali's wit and obvious intelligence, it was hard to believe that his mental abilities were considered inadequate for army service. But few realized that his minimal reading level and virtually nonexistent math and science skills were accurately reflected in the test results. Consider a typical test question:

A vendor was selling apples for $10 a basket. How much would you pay for a dozen baskets if one-third of the apples had been removed from each of the baskets? (a) $10 (b) $30 (c) $40 (d) $80.

"I didn't even know how to start finding the answers," Ali said later.

With all the controversy that swirled around Ali, boxing was temporarily forgotten. A logical rematch with Liston was man-

THE NATION OF ISLAM

ALI WITH A GROUP OF
MUSLIM WOMEN, 1966.

It was in the Detroit ghetto of 1930 that Elijah (Muhammad) Poole met one W. D. Fard, a man with a small group of followers who were transfixed by his mystical stories of an ancient black heritage. For three years, Poole and his wife served as avid disciples until one day Poole asked Fard, "Who are you?" Answered Fard, "I am the one the world has been waiting for the past two thousand years. I have come to guide you unto the right path."

In brief, the general core of Fard's doctrine: Seventy trillion years ago, a black God created the universe. Some six thousand years ago, the peaceful civilization surrounding the all-black holy city of Mecca was disturbed by a large-headed evil scientist named Mr. Yacub, who preached against Allah. Exiled to an island (Patmos) with his 59,999 followers, Yacub, who lived to be 152, swore revenge. Through genetic mutation he created a lighter-skinned people who over six hundred years gradually devolved into a white, blue-eyed race destined to enslave blacks. The evil behavior of the whites caused them to be exiled to Europe, where they continued their savage ways.

Fard's curious history further held that some two thousand years later, Allah sent Moses to civilize the white devils, who in turn were scheduled to dominate for six thousand more years. At that time a black Messiah would arrive to deliver his people from the apocalypse that awaited from a huge mothership hovering over the earth. Enter Fard, who claimed to be that holy man, sent to America to find (or at least to found) the Lost Nation of Islam—the group one day to be disparaged in the press as "Black Muslims."

Fard mysteriously disappeared in 1934, leaving behind Elijah Muhammad as his divine "messenger" to educate and emancipate American blacks. Muhammad moved to Chicago, where he opened the sect's second temple, but in 1942 he was sent to prison for encouraging his followers to defy the draft. Paroled in 1946, Muhammad reestablished his leadership, and by the early 1960s the movement—fueled by the charismatic ascendance of Malcolm X—had grown from a mere few hundred to an estimated sixty thousand members.

As Muhammad's chief lieutenant, ex-convict and reformed drug dealer Malcolm X recruited legions of disaffected blacks to the Nation with fiery oratory heard over the radio and at rallies and press conferences. The gist of the message, as laid forth by his superior, was that blacks should not be bound to a corrupt white society but rather break free and create a separate, morally just society based on their own identity. As a religion, the Nation of Islam offered an antidote to "white" Christianity; as an economic base, it stressed self-sufficiency and trade among blacks; as a social force, it promoted black self-pride and unity.

Malcolm X split from the Nation of Islam in 1964 and was assassinated in 1965. Elijah Muhammad died ten years later. His son Wallace took over leadership of the sect and continued a shift towards orthodox Islam which had begun in the early seventies. Whites were no longer demonized, the Harlem temple was renamed after Malcolm X, and the group itself became the World Community of al-Islam in the West (WCIW).

In the wake of these changes, Minister Louis Farrakhan left the WCIW in 1978 and reconstituted the Nation of Islam, along with many of its old beliefs. Under Farrakhan's leadership, the Nation of Islam once again became a visible and highly controversial religious organization. Ali, though, remained with the WCIW and Wallace Muhammad. In 1984, Ali said of Farrakhan's teachings, "What he teaches is not at all what we believe in. . . . We say he represents the time of our struggle in the dark and a time of confusion in us and we don't want to be associated with that at all."

dated by contract, but now the former champion was having his own problems with investigations into alleged underworld connections. As a respite from all the turmoil, Muhammad Ali was persuaded by friends to tour Africa that spring. These were to be his first steps in what would ultimately turn into a lifetime of international travel as an unofficial ambassador of American Islam. Accompanying him were his brother Rahaman; a Muslim adviser named Archie Robinson (Osman Karriem); Los Angeles photographer Howard Bingham, who, three decades later, would remain the closest of Ali's friends; and Herbert Muhammad, Elijah's son, who was sent along expressly to keep the champ in close tow and who would ultimately become Ali's permanent manager.

Throughout the five-week trip, Ali regaled in his new status as world champion—shaking hands with dignitaries, kissing babies, and clowning with fans across the continent. Public adulation may have been absent on his native soil, but overseas he was a hero. Osman Karriem recalled in Hauser's *Muhammad Ali* how Ali was "hypnotized" as people emerged on a remote road in Ghana to scream his name: "Do you have any idea what it must have been like for him to see thousands of people materialize out of nowhere and know they were there just for him? That day I saw the birth of a new human being. It was like Cassius Clay came to an end and Muhammad Ali emerged."

❧ ❧ ❧

"Get up and fight!"

Shortly after Ali's return from Africa he was introduced by Herbert Muhammad to Sonji Roi, a stunning, divorced cocktail waitress/nightclub singer from the South Side of Chicago.

From their first date that night to the day they were married five weeks later (August 14, 1964) the two never left each other's side. There had been a few other girls before in Ali's life, none of whom he'd been intimate with for long. Sonji unleashed a passion within him he never knew existed.

Were it not for Ali's devout faith, they might have been better paired. However devoted and affectionate toward her husband she was, Sonji nevertheless smoked, drank liquor, wore short skirts and cosmetics, and was generally the antithesis of Muslim womanhood—a fact that would soon wear on not just Ali, but also on those who would influence him. She would wipe off the makeup and change to long dresses for her hus-

i with Sonji Roi.

← ALI AND THE PRESS ←

Much of the public indignation aimed at Muhammad Ali—both before and after his Muslim pronouncements—was fueled by the opinions of old-guard sportswriters of the day. For his part, Ali knew as well as those who covered him how to sell papers. Yet most of the same reporters who benefited from the wealth of material very much resented the source. Ali's emergence would gradually change how athletes dealt with the press, but at the start, his arrogance grated on those with clear-cut opinions of how a champion should comport himself.

Traditionally, boxing press conferences consisted of such mundane queries as "How do you feel today?" and "What did you eat this morning?" Ali, of course, made a shambles of such a process. Wrote celebrated *New Yorker* correspondent A. J. Liebling, "There was a limitless demand for his verse, which saved sportswriters who interviewed him from having to think up gags of their own." Yet those same scribes would sit frowning while Ali delivered off-the-wall monologues. In his book *The Shadow Box,* George Plimpton recalled the press "staring balefully" as Ali carried on: "It seemed incredible that a smile or two wouldn't show up on a writer's face. It was so wonderfully preposterous."

Conservative, widely read sportswriters such as Red Smith, Dick Young, and Jimmy Cannon were actually more comfortable with the cigar-chomping hoodlum element in boxing (e.g., Liston) than with a clown act they saw as silly or religious ties they felt threatened by. Cannon went so far as to attack Ali's Islamic stance as "the dirtiest in American sports since the Nazis were shilling for Max Schmeling as representative of their vile theories of blood." It didn't help that Ali never seemed to take most sports reporters seriously. Instead of worrying about their opinions or approval, Ali often appeared to be using them as straight men to make jokes that they didn't get.

Two decades later, the mainstream sports press would have totally reversed itself. As veteran fight writer Mike Katz told Ali biographer Thomas Hauser: "I guess it's common for sportswriters—and I put myself in the group—to lull ourselves into thinking we're smarter than the athletes we cover. Ali was one of those wonderful people who, every now and then, remind us that, hey, this guy is sharper than we are."

band's sake, but in the end she repeatedly questioned the beliefs and insisted on being her own woman.

"Having a Messenger of God over him," Sonji Roi explained in *The Greatest*, " . . . this thing of having someone above my own man as his leader and teacher . . . I could never accept making another man happy outside of my husband. I wanted no man to tell my husband what to make me do."

For the year that they were together, Ali and Sonji fought regularly, mostly over religion and lifestyle. There was even one very public squabble over a low-cut dress that nearly resulted in Ali's squaring off with his idol Sugar Ray Robinson, who'd risen to Sonji's defense. Their marriage would last barely a year; that it lasted officially as long as it did was due to Ali's not wanting his preparations for the upcoming Liston rematch—set for November 19 in Boston—to be disrupted in any way.

Despite his having ballooned in weight during the months away from boxing—a trend that would plague his entire career—Muhammad Ali trained himself back to a superb condition for Liston that fall. His weight was back down to 210 pounds, he had grown half an inch to 6 feet, 3 inches, his waist was still 34, and his biceps and thighs had expanded 2 inches.

But three days before the scheduled Ali/Clay-Liston II, Ali began to feel sick while watching television. After extensive vomiting, he was rushed to a Boston hospital, where he underwent one hour of emergency surgery for a hernia. The condition was described as congenital by doctors, but Liston saw it differently: "If he'd stop all that hollering, he wouldn't have a hernia."

At any rate, the match was postponed for six months, during which time the Massachusetts boxing authorities refused sanctioning, due to Liston's alleged crime connections. After considerable head-scratching, a new site was found, this time a skating rink/youth center in remote Lewiston, Maine. The delay was enough time for Liston's own conditioning to deteriorate ominously. Some fight people even thought he was using heroin at the same time he was training.

On February 25, 1965, Malcolm X was assassinated by gunmen at a rally in Harlem. The shooting was believed by many at the time to have been ordered by Elijah Muhammad. The fallout from the killing (and a mysterious fire that gutted Ali's Chicago apartment that same night) would reach all the way to the champion's training camp and contribute to an already wild atmosphere surrounding the rematch. In Maine, Ali was blanketed around-the-clock by elite Nation of Islam bodyguards as rumors of attempts on his life circulated freely in the weeks before the bout. Seeking to sell more seats, one of the promoters took out a well-publicized million-dollar life insurance policy on Ali. The fight went off, barely, before a sparse crowd of twenty-five hundred fans. Despite his earlier defeat, Liston was the nine-to-five betting favorite. Those who bet big money out of Vegas still didn't believe in Ali.

And many still wouldn't after the ensuing one-round stunner. The fight is primarily remembered for Ali's "phantom" punch that dropped Liston, but in reality there were three punches that effected the result. The first was a right cross that backed Liston in his tracks; the second, a debilitating right on the temple. The third, with Sonny in desperate trouble, was yet another right, delivered with sleight-of-hand speed and enough power to lift Liston off the canvas.

Exacerbating the sudden ending—fans screamed "Fake!" and "Fix!" as Liston lay on his back—was the confusion surrounding novice referee Jersey Joe Walcott's long count. Rather than return to a neutral corner, Ali stood over the fallen Liston, screaming at him, "Get up and fight!" Struggling with Ali, Walcott took forever trying to count the challenger out, who at one point arose and groggily took a fighting stance. Walcott then raised Ali's hand as the winner, forty-two seconds after the knockdown.

Decades later, Ali explained his own frustrations to the end of the Liston rematch: "People said the first fight was fixed, so the second time I wanted to whup him bad. I didn't want him making excuses or quitting. I wanted him to get up so I could show everybody how great I was."

London, 1966

CHAPTER FOUR

"WHAT'S MY NAME?"

————◆————

I have nothing but contempt for the Black Muslims and that for which they stand," railed Floyd Patterson in a lengthy *Sports Illustrated* diatribe that appeared a few months following the Ali-Liston rematch. "Cassius Clay must be beaten and the Black Muslims' scourge removed from boxing."

While so much of pro boxing's ritual posturing can be passed off as hype and promotion, Patterson's gauntlet was disturbingly sincere. Here was a man who, after literally going into hiding following his second loss to Liston (he wore disguises in public), had emerged to become the most vocal of Ali's detractors. Possibly his five straight wins gave him the confidence necessary for what he called his "moral crusade." Whatever. With Liston all but forgotten, Patterson provided Ali with a convenient foil. Calling him an "Uncle Tom" and dubbing him "the rabbit" ("because he's scared"), Ali took Patterson's bait with a vengeance.

The buildup to their November 22, 1965, fight in Las Vegas began innocently enough, with Ali appearing at Patterson's training camp waving a head of lettuce and a bunch of carrots. But Ali's usual playful side was noticeably absent as the prefight rhetoric gradually turned vindictive and ugly. Calling Patterson a "deaf-dumb Negro who needs a good spanking," Ali said he planned "to punish him for the things he's said about me in magazines. . . . I want to see him cut, his ribs caved in, and then knocked out."

As repugnant as Ali's black militant stance may have been to Patterson, so, too, were Patterson's integrationist views to Ali. In a sense, the bout took on a socioreligious angle as both fighters headed for the ring spurred on by their beliefs. After learning of Patterson's expulsion from a white suburb, Ali once again put his thoughts to verse:

> *I'm gonna put him flat on his back*
> *So that he will start acting black.*
> *Because when he was champ he didn't do as he should*
> *He tried to force himself into an all-white neighbor*
> *hood.*

However misguided Patterson's patriotic goals, however spiteful Ali's reactions, few among the eight thousand fans who braved a rare desert torrential downpour were quite prepared for the cruel spectacle that awaited them. In the opening round, Ali, without throwing a single punch, danced disdainfully around Patterson, who plodded awkwardly forward in his trademark arms-high "peekaboo" style. From then on, Ali thoroughly dominated Patterson, battering his adversary with intermittent barrages, toying with him by easing up, only to follow with additional punishment. Each time a knockout seemed imminent, Ali

ALI'S RING STYLE

Throughout the early part of Muhammad Ali's career, boxing purists were quick to point out three glaring "flaws": (1) Ali, of course, held his hands at his sides most of the time—a no-no for the art of self-defense, in the sense of how can one get the hands up to block punches?; (2) he pulled his head straight back to avoid punches, rather than "slip" them by ducking side-to-side; (3) he always circled clockwise.

Fair enough, said Ali, to criticism he'd heard as far back as his Golden Gloves days. But at the height of his game, he knew that sheer speed and reflexes would obviate any need for a standard defensive technique. As the great trainer Eddie Futch once put it: "He had so much ability he could outrun his mistakes."

The hands held low allowed Ali to hook without having to pull the arm back, as well as provided a starting point for flash uppercuts. The "unprotected" stance enticed fighters to come in closer, where they'd become easier targets. As for leaning back, the combination of phenomenal leg speed and a sort of punch "radar" made Ali impossible to hit (except when the speed was gone late in his career).

Even though Ali stood alone as a boxing innovator, his style, so reliant on speed, was virtually inimitable. For example, he considered the standard retreat of sliding first right then left foot back as inferior, preferring instead a fast backward shuffle on the toes, which allowed him to "float like a butterfly."

Perfect timing and full extension of punches enhanced the wizardry. A stroboscopic camera once timed Ali releasing a six-punch combination in 2.15 seconds from opening left jab to final explosive right to the head. Throw in strength and stamina, the ability to improvise and outthink adversaries in nanoseconds, and an obvious relish for psychological battle, and you have the components for boxing genius.

Ali's most famous style innovation of his later years, the "rope-a-dope," though not the most attractive strategy, brought him what may have been his most dramatic win, over George Foreman in Zaire. Without telling anyone in his corner, Ali decided that he would cover up and lean back on the ropes for the early rounds, letting the hard-hitting Foreman tire himself out. In the eighth, after a weary barrage from Foreman, a rested Ali shot forward and knocked out the champion with a four-punch combination.

would step back to prolong the torture. It was to no avail that Angelo Dundee, in the twelfth, yelled, "Ali, knock him out, for chrissake!" Finally the fight was mercifully halted two minutes into that round by referee Harry Krause, who'd seen enough. So had the crowd, as they jeered the victor.

Ali claimed afterward that he wasn't "carrying" Patterson, who he insisted took his best punches and "wouldn't fall." Critics wouldn't buy it—not Joe Louis, who called Ali "selfish and cruel" for "putting on a show," nor even one of Ali's usually most ardent supporters, *The New York Times*'s Robert Lipsyte, who equated the champion's behavior to "a little boy pulling off the wings of a butterfly piecemeal." In the ring after the fight, Ali seemed to welcome any controversy. "Patterson was fighting for you folks," he mock-intoned to the cameras. "They can't talk about you, Floyd. You're the good, clean American, and I'm that bad Muslim."

"No Vietcong ever called me 'nigger'!"

The year 1966 started in lousy fashion for the heavyweight champion of the world. To begin with, the marriage with Sonji was dissolved on January 7 in a Miami court, a proceeding that included public testimony baring what Ali considered irreparable grounds for divorce: She refused to wear long Muslim dresses. Sonji said she loved him dearly but could not get with the program. "It's just this religion," she told friends afterward. "I have tried to accept this and I have explained this to him, but I just don't understand it."

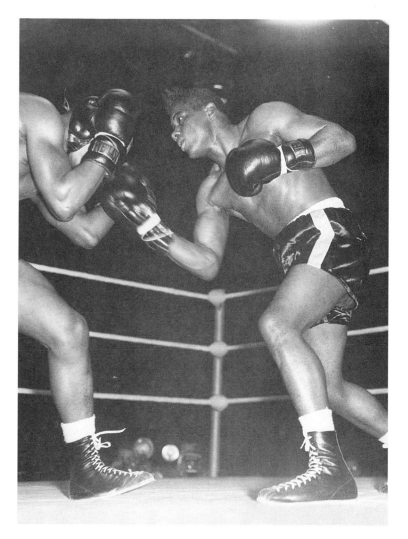

Floyd Patterson in action.

A month after Ali's divorce, the army, needing bodies for the Vietnam War, lowered its standards on the mental aptitude test he had failed two years earlier. Ali, who'd been sorely embarrassed by the earlier contretemps ("they told everybody I was a

☞ TRAINING ☜

WORKING WITH THE HEAVY BAG, 1966.

That Ali fought so well so often in what for him were difficult times owed greatly to the personal discipline he brought to training camp. There were no great secrets to his routine, which was fairly traditional as far as boxing standards go. He loved his body and he loved to train.

The day would always begin with a predawn run of three to five miles, the distance and speed depending on stages of conditioning. He would intermittently run backward or skip sideways for stretches to build up different muscles, careful to avoid getting overtired, which could seriously drain ring stamina in the long run. After roadwork, Ali would drink tea or juice, then go back to sleep until late morning, when he'd get up for his daily ring work.

The noontime gym session would typically start with stretching, followed usually by five separate stages of an approximately two-hour workout: jump rope, speed bag, heavy bag, sparring, and exercises. Skipping rope built up the legs, punching the speed bag maintained timing and coordination (and the muscles for holding the arms aloft), and hitting the heavy bag developed punching power and ring movement. With Ali, sparring was an art form, a chance for him to work on his balletic moves against carefully selected partners. Grueling abdominal and neck exercises ended the workouts, always under the vigilant eye of Ali's conditioning guru Luis Sarria, who also served as personal masseur. Workouts were followed by balanced meals prepared by camp cook Lana Shabazz, who for years watched over Ali's diet.

In the old days, trainers insisted that their fighters abstain from sex during training, the better to conserve strength and aggression. That such ideas are today considered irrelevant must in some part be due to a standard set by Ali. An innocent babe in the early years, he later made up for lost time with a gargantuan sexual appetite—often seeing several different women in any single afternoon. Safe to say, it had little effect on his ring performance.

nut"), was now declared eligible for induction. Upon learning the news in Miami, he grew increasingly unnerved as reporters hounded him all day for his reaction. Finally, he capped one phone exchange with the now-classic comment that would appear everywhere as the next day's headline: "Man, I ain't got no quarrel with them Vietcong."

Press reaction was swift, furious, and even goofy. Red Smith wrote, "Cassius makes himself as sorry a spectacle as those unwashed punks who picket and demonstrate against the war." Milton Gross opined, "As a man, he cannot compare to some of the kids slogging through rice paddies where the names are stranger than Muhammad Ali." Jimmy Cannon looped Ali in with "painters who copy the labels off soup cans and the surf bums who refuse to work and the whole pampered style-making cult of the young."

Yet given that antiwar sentiment was in its seminal stages in 1966, Ali's was a prescient voice of protest. On the same day of the "quarrel" quote, General Maxwell Taylor admonished Senator Wayne Morse for aiding the enemy by opposing the war. For his part, Ali would make matters even worse by clarifying his earlier comment thusly: "No Vietcong ever called me 'nigger'!"

Ali's pronouncements had a decided negative effect on his immediate boxing future. An anticipated bout scheduled for March in Chicago with Ernie Terrell (champion of the lightly regarded World Boxing Association) was refused by the Illinois Athletic Commission, which cited violations of an obscure "Illinois Sports Act." When Louisville was sought as a possible alternative, the Kentucky State Senate officially condemned Ali. Other venues fell through as politicians in various states joined the chorus. The promoters eventually found Toronto as a grudging host, but by then Terrell backed out, allegedly fearing a gate boycott that would reduce his percentage deal to practically nothing. Cynical insiders pointed out that Terrell, a likely loser, was probably gambling on regaining his belt (however bogus) by default once Ali got banned from professional boxing. At any rate, Canadian champion George Chuvalo accepted the fight on three weeks' notice.

Even though it was held across the Canadian border, the beleaguered event would suffer at the gate from the effects of public opinion back home. Popular former heavyweight contender Billy Conn blurted to reporters, "Any American who pays to see him [Ali] fight should feel ashamed." Pennsylvania representative Frank Clark told Congress Ali turned his stomach and urged "the citizens of the nation as a whole to boycott any of his performances." Under pressure from the VFW and the American Legion, closed-circuit venues—then a huge part of prizefight profits—broke loose from the fight; once projected as a million-dollar take, Ali's earnings for the fight would barely cover expenses.

Called "the washerwoman" by Ali for his arms-flailing style, George Chuvalo was a journeyman fighter best known for the fact that he had never been knocked down. Chuvalo was truly a straightforward plodder, and his favorite weapon was described by one ring veteran as a "left chin to the right hand." Against Ali, Chuvalo's street-tough, persevering style served only to absorb an unfathomable amount of punches to the face over fifteen full losing rounds. The best that could be gleaned from Ali's third successful heavyweight title defense was that Chuvalo's record of remaining upright was still intact. Ali was still undefeated, but his earning power was seriously in jeopardy. According to future promoter Bob Arum (then in charge of closed-circuit telecasts), "Clay in the United States is a dead piece of merchandise."

"... boxing will be a graveyard."

Back home, Ali's draft case worked its way through the early appeal stages of a lengthy legal journey. His attorneys contended that he should be deferred for any of three reasons: (1) conscientious objection; (2) religious grounds; or (3) he would lose the ability to support his family. Meanwhile, the federal government responded to the hue and cry of Ali's "antipatriotism" by launching an extensive FBI investigation of Ali's background.

As Ali's Stateside prospects grew dimmer by the hour, the champion and his advisers—now mostly Muslims (the Louisville sponsorship group was gradually being phased out)—turned to a series of lucrative fight offers overseas. With the expenses of his growing entourage, with his hefty alimony payments, and with his 70 percent income-tax bracket, Ali, who only a short time earlier had seemingly been rolling in dough, was suddenly teetering toward cash poverty. The obvious choice and best draw was Henry Cooper, the Englishman who had nearly KO'd Ali in London three years earlier. The fight loomed as a blockbuster—the first heavyweight title bout in England since 1908.

This time around, Ali was ever the gentleman, at every occasion praising both his "worthy opponent" and the British people, who as a whole were indifferent to his affiliations back home. The fight was the biggest in Anglo history; excitement rose to a fever pitch when the forty-two thousand Cooper faithful packed the Arsenal soccer stadium to cheer on their ten-

to-one underdog favorite son. But for all his grit (and dangerous hook), the former plasterer was once again outclassed. For
five rounds Ali, who confessed beforehand that he hated
blood, managed to avoid hitting Cooper's eyebrows. Then in
the sixth, he caught the Brit with a chopping right hand that
opened a sickening gusher near the left brow. Fight over.
"Blood scares me," said Ali afterward, thankful the fight had
been stopped. "I was more desperate than anyone else when I
saw him bleeding so badly."

Though Ali was fighting overseas, it was now easier for Americans to watch him fight than it ever had been. ABC Sports,
under the leadership of Roone Arledge, had begun to experi-

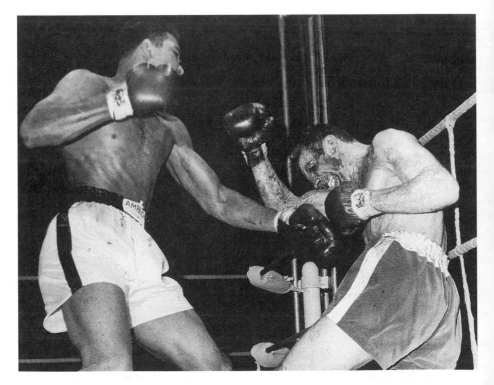

Ali-Cooper II ended in the sixth round, after a cut over Cooper's left eye.

ment with new approaches to covering sporting events and sports in general. The emphasis was not on simply showing the event but rather on presenting it as a spectacle, drawing the viewer in and heightening the drama, and Muhammad Ali was a perfect athlete with which to create drama. After seeing how well rebroadcasts of his fights had done in the ratings, ABC had bought the rights to telecast live Ali's three title defenses with Cooper, London, and Mildenberger subsequent to the Chuvalo fight. Rather than put one camera on the ring at the start of the fight and let the action take place, ABC packaged the bouts as something more than just boxing matches, wrapping musical introductions, interviews, and other feature material around the fight. Ali in turn realized the value of ABC's involvement to his career. As well as engaging in his well-known on-camera relationship with Howard Cosell, Ali played along in other ways to help ABC. At the Cooper fight, the last match on the undercard ended much sooner than the network had foreseen, bringing up the main event eighteen minutes before ABC wanted it for its live broadcast. Cosell went to Ali's dressing room and asked the champion for help. Though according to the British boxing officials, the fighters had two minutes to enter the ring, Ali did not show up until the eighteen minutes had passed.

Despite the national letdown of the Cooper loss, British promoters had another offer at the ready for Ali—an August 6 bout against the suspect Brian London (the "Blackpool Bulldog"), a fighter thrice beaten by Cooper. Ali accepted what turned out to be a ludicrously easy outing, despite some minimal training and obvious preoccupation with his situation in the States ("a champion fighting on two fronts," reported *The London Daily Mirror*). A rapid-fire, third-round flurry sent London sliding to the canvas in what critics felt was an all-too-easy $100,000 payday. "A lamb trying to bite a dog!" wrote one native pressman of the fight. "His punches made me dizzy," was how London assessed it.

On both trips to England Ali was accompanied by Herbert Muhammad, son of Elijah: Herbert was destined to earn countless millions of dollars as Ali's boxing manager. "People like Queen Elizabeth, Khrushchev, they have advisers," said Ali, explaining Herbert's presence in London. "That's my brains right there." The contract with the all-white Louisville sporting group was nearing its end and would not be renewed. Much was said and written at the time about control of the champion being wrested from those who had his best interests in mind, but in fact, Muhammad Ali would earn far more proportionally under the vigilance of Herbert than he ever had under Bill Faversham, who basically ran the group. "We know it's a crooked business," said Elijah Muhammad at the time, "but we want Muhammad to get justice out of it."

On August 23, Ali appeared in person at a special draft hearing on his status. Allowing that Ali was "sincere in his objection on religious grounds to participation in war in any form," the hearing officer, a retired Kentucky judge, recommended conscientious objector status to the Appeals Board. But the federal Justice Department countered the opinion by claiming that their FBI investigation showed Ali was not serious in his convictions and that his objections to war were political, not religious. Despite Ali's lawyer's new claim that his client was an ordained Muslim minister, the appeal was refused.

On September 10 Ali was back overseas to fight German Karl Mildenberger in Frankfurt. In the midst of what was turning into a busy year of fighting, Ali suffered a mild letdown against a game opponent with a confusing southpaw lead (right jab). Never in risk of actually losing, the champion nonetheless

◆ HOWARD COSELL ◆

COSELL'S CAREER WAS GREATLY AIDED BY THE ATTENTION BROUGHT TO IT BY ALI.

Of Muhammad Ali's few defenders at the time of his draft problems and ensuing exile, none was more vehement than broadcaster Howard Cosell. A former lawyer, the controversial Cosell voiced strong support of Ali's constitutional rights as a conscientious objector and long before that was the first to recognize Ali's rightful name change. From his autobiography *Cosell:* "Muhammad Ali knew that I was on the side of justice. I could not have cared less what the public's reaction would be toward me, and in some corners of the country I was already labeled a 'White Muslim.'"

Ali and Cosell struck up a mutually beneficial relationship early in both of their careers. Ali had long known the benefits of a direct line to the public via television, and Cosell was quick to see how performing as Ali's straight man in their interviews furthered his own stature. Their's was an odd, slapsticky on-air pairing that somehow got over—Cosell challenging Ali on some point or another, the latter answering back with a quip, a face, a rhyme, or even a mock hint of potential violence ("I'm gonna whup you, Cosell").

Ali liked and respected Cosell, yet he has often let it be known that Cosell rode his coattails to fame and should not forget it. Once in the middle of a round, Ali admonished Cosell through the ropes for something the broadcaster had said. In another instance he complimented Cosell on "Wide World of Sports" for not being "as dumb as he looked." In his book, Cosell characterized Ali as "a mercurial man, impenetrable, a man who will always puzzle and confuse me. But, always, a salesman." If he had cared enough, Ali would probably have said the same of Cosell.

required twelve difficult rounds before he could effectively "solve" the situation with a stunning standing TKO of the bleeding German, who'd twice been down in earlier rounds. Lending some irony to the evening were the five thousand GI's sitting in the cheaps to cheer or jeer their nation's most famous draft dodger. The fight was also the first live transatlantic telecast to be transmitted in color by Telstar satellite.

Ali's fifth and final fight of 1966 took place in November in the Houston Astrodome against Cleveland "Big Cat" Williams, one of the toughest, hardest-punching heavyweights of the 1960s. Quick to overlook Ali's problems, the state of Texas was hoping to host an upset by its native son (whom Ali took to calling "Pussycat"). That would leave a "world rid of the biggest mouth in boxing," as Williams' oil baron manager, Hugh Benbow, put it. But only in their wildest dreams could anyone beat Ali at his best, and against Williams that night, Ali was at his very best. As promised, he unveiled his little quick-step "Ali shuffle," adding substance with thunderous left-right combinations that resulted in four devastating knockdowns. Williams staggered to his feet each time, but as he floundered about the ring one minute into the third round, the referee mercifully stopped it. The awesome display of punching power left many to wonder if there existed anyone capable of giving Ali a tussle—save, of course, the U.S. government.

His draft problems still unresolved, Ali returned to the Astrodome in early 1967 for the once-heralded match with Ernie Terrell. Again, as with Patterson, there was bad blood stemming from Terrell's pointed insistence on addressing the champion as Cassius. Terrell would later insist he did so as "part of the promotion," but as Ali's former sparring partner, he knew of the champ's deep convictions—Ali had even once tried to convert him to Islam. For such lack of respect, Ali vowed to make Terrell pay: "I want to torture him. A clean knockout is too good for him."

And so it was again ugly. After a relatively close fight in the early going, Ali established clear superiority with superb boxing skills, then sullied the same with his cruelty. In the eighth round, with the challenger's eyes nearly swollen shut, Ali circled and popped Terrell at will, alternately easing up and taunting him with "What's my name?" and calling him "Uncle Tom." From the tenth on, Ali did appear to try to end it, but he was by then too arm-weary to do so, even though Terrell posed no threat whatsoever. Ali won a unanimous fifteen-round decision; Terrell was taken to the hospital for emergency eye surgery. A typical reaction to Ali's display came from *The New York Daily News*'s Gene Ward, who called the fight "an open defiance of decency, sportsmanship, and all the tenets of right versus wrong."

As if desperate for another payday before the government's clock struck twelve, Ali signed for a fight with number one contender Zora Folley in Madison Square Garden, set for a mere five weeks after Terrell. It would be Ali's seventh title defense in the past twelve months, over which time he'd grossed nearly $2 million. Just ten days before the Folley fight, Ali received an official notice asking him to report for induction on April 11 in Louisville (the date was extended two weeks and changed to Houston). Ali gave ticket sales a big boost by warning, "This may be the last chance to see Muhammad Ali in living color."

Ali had said following the Terrell fight that the boy who would eventually beat him was now ten years old. Unfortunately, Folley, whom Ali termed a "civilized, respectable" man, was now thirty-four, an advanced age for a boxer. For the first three rounds, Ali waltzed in perpetual motion around Folley, who looked frozen in time. In the fourth, the champion downshifted, sat back on his heels, and rocked a chopping right that flopped Folley to the floor. The challenger arose and survived until the seventh, when Ali threw two devastating short rights that brought the end. "He could write the book on boxing," said Folley afterward, "and anyone that fights him should be made to read it first." But for Ali, there would be no more fights for three and a half years. "After I go," he had said a few nights earlier, "boxing will be a graveyard."

"I refuse to be inducted."

On April 28, 1967, Muhammad Ali appeared at the appointed hour in Houston, firm in his resolve to stand behind his beliefs. Many wondered why he didn't just allow himself to be drafted, box exhibitions for the army, and be done with it. But over and over, he spelled out the previous example of Elijah Muhammad's years in prison and how it was not permitted for Muslims to partake in any way in any war not ordained by the Holy Qur'an (Koran). "I am the tool of Allah," said Ali, "and because of my sacrifice it will come out that hundreds of Muslims are in jail rather than fight in the army."

Outside the induction center, a handful of demonstrators milled around with signs that read, "Draft beer, not Ali" and "Ali, stay home." Inside the building, the morning went by with routine processing and tests. Around one o'clock, the names of inductees were individually called (there were twenty-six in the group) and asked to step forward. Ali refused, offering, as requested, a brief written statement that gave his reason: "I refuse to be inducted into the armed forces of the United States because I claim to a minister of the religion of Islam."

No immediate action was taken by the Department of Justice or the Selective Service System; that would come later. Ali proceeded to a media room where he gave out copies of a four-page statement that included the following: "My decision is a private and individual one. In taking it I am dependent solely upon Allah as the final judge of these actions brought about by my own conscience. I strongly object to the fact that so many newspapers have given the American public and the world the impression that I have only two alternatives in taking this stand—either I go to jail or go to the army. There is another alternative, and that alternative is justice."

Chicago, 1966

CHAPTER FIVE

THE MOST FAMOUS MAN

---◆---

Barely an hour after Muhammad Ali refused induction into the U.S. Army, the New York State Athletic Commission suspended his boxing license and refused to recognize him as the world heavyweight champion—this before he had even been charged with violating any federal law. Shortly afterward, the other states and boxing organizations fell in line, effectively blackballing Ali from his chosen profession. Corrupt ruling bodies play a large part in professional boxing's checkered history; that they rose collectively under the cloak of patriotism to condemn their brightest star stands as a fitting testament to their own sorry record over the years.

If Ali stood firm in his resolve ("Allah okays the adversary to try us," he would tell sympathizers, "that's how he sees if you're a believer"), so, too, did the forces against him. Ten days after his act of defiance, he was indicted by a federal grand jury for unlawfully refusing induction (he pleaded not guilty). Two months later he was tried, convicted, and sentenced to the maximum: five years in prison and a $10,000 fine. Judge Joe Ingraham ruled at the trial that the court was not empowered to consider the defendant's ministerial claims. Naturally, Ali would appeal, but for now his world continued to crumble. One of his less scintillating poetic efforts summed up his mood:

> *Clean out my cell*
> *And take my tail*
> *On the trail*
> *For the jail*
> *Without bail*
> *Because it's better in jail*
> *Watchin' television fed*
> *Than in Vietnam somewhere dead*

Such was the lighter side to Ali's feelings about what lay ahead. At other times the mercurial ex-champ was alternately somber and angry. "Step into a billion dollars and denounce my people or step into poverty and teach them the truth," he railed at a group of prominent black athletes trying to get him to accept the military. "Damn the money. Damn the heavyweight championship. Damn the white people. Damn everything. I will die before I sell out my people for the white man's money."

The fact is, Ali could have chosen an obvious easier way out of his predicament. Like Joe Louis during World War II, he could very well have put on the uniform, allowed himself to be photographed a zillion times for troop morale, and boxed exhibitions along the way. With but token service for Uncle Sam, his career would have remained relatively intact at the same

NEW YORK STATE ATHLETIC COMMISSION

The fight game has always been regulated ... sort of. Every so often a call is heard for the formation of a federal agency to oversee boxing, but thus far the sport has seen fit to police itself via state commissions whose functions range from licensing boxers, managers, and promoters, to on-site medical supervision, to officiating, etc. The New York commission is one of the oldest of these agencies, though rarely—as evidenced by the Ali debacle—the wisest.

At the time of Ali's draft evasion, the commission was chaired by Edwin Dooley, a former college football hero and congressman and a political appointee of Nelson Rockefeller's. At Ali's fateful hour, Dooley had left his minions with four different press releases based on the variety of scenarios that might take place. When Ali took his stand, Dooley, on phone hookup to Houston, immediately ordered that the champion be stripped of his title and of the right to earn his living in New York. One by one, the other state commissions followed suit.

Incredibly, the chance that Ali might ever be found not guilty made

ALI CLAIMING CONSCIENTOUS-
OBJECTOR STATUS, 1967.

little difference to Dooley, nor to the other commissions across the country, who allowed any number of ex-cons and felons into their rings through the years. Almost four years later, Ali was cleared to fight in New York, but only after his lawyers presented a federal district court with a list of ninety boxers who—despite convictions of crimes ranging from murder to child molestation to military desertion—were at the time licensed to box in the state.

time that he'd have been ridding himself of costly negative press. But the fact remains that Ali took a strong personal stand on grounds that, in retrospect, hold up magnificently. He was headed to jail merely for opposing the most misguided military effort in American history, a war that killed tens of thousands of young blacks routinely sent to the front lines in numbers disproportionate to those of whites. Ali could have kept his title and earning powers even while in uniform. Instead, he threw it all away for principles that are universally accepted today. Said Hall of Fame basketballer Bill Russell at the time: "I still envy him. He has something I have never been able to attain and very few people I know possess. He has an absolute and sincere faith."

While in exile, Ali's image would gradually recover. The year 1967 was a seminal one of antiwar protest and one during which the ex-champion, by circumstance, became one of the movement's heroes. White liberals who spearheaded the cause held Ali up as a political and religious martyr victimized by a corrupt power structure. (Mindful of Elijah Muhammad's disdain for "white man's politics," Ali, however, kept a safe distance from any organizations.) At the same time, boxing's staunch old guard quickly sought a new heavyweight titleholder. Their efforts only served to entrench Ali in the interim as the proverbial "people's champ."

An elimination tournament that featured an assortment of Ali's past victims and sparring partners was hastily organized by the World Boxing Association. Ali's future antagonist Joe Frazier refused to participate; Sonny Liston wasn't invited. Ali's view at the time: "Let the man who wins go to the backwoods of Georgia and Alabama or Sweden or Africa, let him say 'What's my name?' and see what they say. Everybody knows me and knows I am the champion." Ali's former spar-

With Belinda Boyd, 1969.

ring partner, Jimmy Ellis, won the sham tourney title over Leo-
tis Martin on August 6. Some six months later, at Madison
Square Garden, Frazier beat Buster Mathis for an equally
fraudulent New York "world title." Inside the arena, fight fans
struck up a chant that would haunt Frazier's championship
years: "A-li! A-li!" Outside the arena, antiwar protesters held
up posters of the fallen champion.

In the summer of 1967, Ali appeared as a guest speaker at
the University of Islam in Chicago, where he was smitten by
Belinda Boyd, a seventeen-year-old Muslim girl he'd met six
years earlier. Belinda, who worked in a Muslim bakery, was tall,
bright, beautiful, and devoutly religious. They were married on

COMPUTER TOURNAMENT

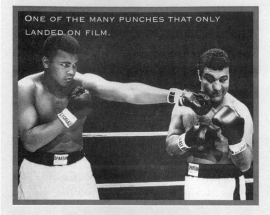

ONE OF THE MANY PUNCHES THAT ONLY LANDED ON FILM.

In the midst of Ali's boxing exile, an advertising man named Murray Woroner came up with an idea for a fictitious computer-based boxing tournament of past heavyweight champions to be broadcast on radio. Rocky Marciano was the ultimate winner of a questionable series that had Ali somehow losing to Jim Jeffries in the first round. Ali wasn't amused and sued for a million dollars. "They won't let me fight to earn a living anymore and my name is all I've got," he said. "Now someone is trying to ruin that, too."

But Woroner persuaded Ali to drop the lawsuit when he came up with another brainstorm—a filmed, choreographed "bout" between Ali and Marciano, for which both would be well paid. Balding, overweight, and thirteen years retired, Marciano trained hard and donned a wig for the filming. Ali laughed his way through the seventy-five one-minute rounds shot from a variety of angles, although he did feel the brunt of some body punches Marciano let fly, somewhat in disrespect of the staged proceedings.

Several different endings were filmed—both fighters by knockout, both stopped on cuts (fake blood), decisions, etc.—and the entire footage was supposedly analyzed, fed into computers, and edited into a simulated fight for closed-circuit viewing. Despite the knowledge that the entire deal was a setup, fans turned out in decent numbers and saw Ali get "knocked out" in the thirteenth round (the ending was kept secret until the viewing). A week later in England, however, the BBC telecast a different version in which Marciano lost on cuts. "It don't matter," Ali would shrug about the result. "Nobody's gonna believe a movie anyway."

August 16; Maryum, the first of their four children, was born the following June.

Life in a relatively slower lane was a difficult change for Ali, but he adapted well, rising at daybreak to pray (repeated five times daily), spending hours reading the dictionary and studying the Koran, and generally acting as much the family man as his wandering personality would allow. (He would love all his children and lavish them with gifts, but he himself would confess to having little patience for their extended company.) Oftentimes he strolled his Chicago neighborhood or drove his red Caddy around the streets to enjoy shouts of recognition from fans and admirers ("Good luck, champ!"). Years later, Belinda, then divorced from Ali, would recall those days as "happy" ones when they "did without and worked together."

Ever low on funds, Ali began accepting scores of offers to lecture on the college circuit. With the combination of his natural showmanship, his politically correct antiwar sentiments, and his status as the baaadest-man on earth, he became a popular speaker in front of largely white student audiences. Jokingly, he listed "hippies" as his most ardent supporters.

Ali's subjects and sermons were loosely interwoven with his plight, his speeches well prepared beforehand with Belinda's help. He talked, orated, rapped, and preached his way around Islam, black pride, love, hate, integration vs. segregation, boxing, economics, and any number of his views on life. His style was part homespun public speaker, part Muslim proselytizer, part "The Greatest." "Who's the champ?" he would ask his rapt audiences before leaving. "You are!" was the resounding response. Robert Lipsyte told Ali biographer Thomas Hauser that on the speaking tour "Ali was providing a window on a lot of social, political, and religious things that were going on in

America; a window into the black world that wouldn't have been available to his listeners any other way."

In May 1968 the federal Fifth Circuit Court of Appeals upheld Ali's conviction, and the noose appeared to tighten a bit. Essentially, the court ruled that as a professional boxer, Ali's claims to the ministry were dubious, even as he was then regularly preaching at mosques around the country. Ali vowed to seek justice all the way to the U.S. Supreme Court, but his legal bills were mounting rapidly.

His case still on appeal, Muhammad Ali had become a virtual prisoner in his own country. Lucrative bouts abroad in England and Japan ($250,000 in Yokohama) were barred by a federal judge, who ordered Ali's passport confiscated. Even a wild proposal for a one-hour visit to fight across the border in Tijuana was denied. All this time, Ali's associates worked feverishly behind the scenes trying to secure a fight in the States. They came close, but at every potential venue their efforts fell victim to prevailing politics. Once, in Las Vegas, a return match with Floyd Patterson was nearly secured, only to be nixed at the last minute by the governor, who it turned out was getting his orders from Howard Hughes. There were even plans to box on the Gila River Indian reservation until tribal elders decided their "historical heritage" could not allow it. "We worked through a dozen states," recalled Ali's longtime publicist Harold Conrad. "Couldn't move anybody."

Ali seemed reconciled to jail, which he actually experienced in Miami for one week in December 1968—for driving without a valid license. The unexpectedly harsh sentence for such a minor offense seemed little more than a nasty fallout from his greater notoriety. But perhaps the cruelest blow of all during his exile came from the hand of Elijah Muhammad, who in April 1969 suspended Ali from the Nation of Islam.

The suspension stemmed from some public remarks Ali had made about how he would ultimately return to boxing "if the money's right." In Elijah's eyes this amounted to crawling back to the white man to beg for money. In his statement in *Muhammad Speaks,* Elijah claimed that "Mr. Muhammad Ali desired to do that which the Holy Qur'an teaches him against." For such a transgression, Elijah also stripped Ali of his name. Humbly apologetic, Ali would return to the good graces of his leader within a year.

Yet more proof that Ali's name was still marketable, however dubiously, was evidenced by his appearance in November, 1969, in an ill-fated Broadway musical titled *Big Time Buck White*. Ali had previously declined a substantial offer of $400,000 to appear in a film based on Jack Johnson's life, saying that he would not share the screen with a white woman. This time he accepted stagelights, but only after securing a complex contract that allowed him to cut lines he considered morally compromising. The result left a bland offering about slavery that closed after one week. The reviews were generally bad, save for their compliments toward the ex-champ's thespian talents. "He [Ali] sings with a pleasant, slightly impersonal voice, acts without embarrassment, and moves with innate dignity," wrote Clive Barnes in *The New York Times*. "He does himself proud."

While his case wound its way through the courts, Ali trained sporadically. At times he talked of his return to the ring, at other times of his retirement. "I'm through fighting," he announced in a May 1970 *Esquire* profile. "Y'all keep it all. I don't need no prestige at beating up nobody. I'm tired. And I want to be the first black champion that got out that didn't get whipped."

Yet despite his threats to quit the fight game, Ali couldn't resist keeping a keen eye on developments within the heavyweight division. In February, 1970, the two "official" world champions, Jimmy Ellis and Joe Frazier, met in a title unification bout. The totally one-sided contest ended in the fifth round with Ellis flat on his back. As a destructive force, the undefeated Frazier was all of a sudden touted by the press as being in the same league with the pre-Ali Sonny Liston. For his part, Ali showed little patience for the high praise lavished on a man he considered a pretender to his stolen crown. "It might shock and amaze ya," his new catchphrase would go, "but I will destroy Joe Fraz-ier."

With career and life still very much up in the air, Ali nevertheless discovered a new foil in Frazier. Having recently moved to Philadelphia, Frazier's adopted hometown, Ali wasted little time in confronting his future adversary, bugging him repeatedly on the phone, and baiting him in the park, where the two would pass each other during their roadwork. In his autobiography *Keep on Smokin'*, Frazier recalled how, early one morning, he rebuffed Ali's challenge to fight right then and there: "I don't want to waste it in private," he told Ali. "I want the whole world to see what I'm gonna' do to you."

❦   ❦   ❦

". . . no time for poems . . ."

By mid-1970 a clear majority of Americans had turned against the Vietnam War. Richard Nixon's number one priority as president was the task of returning home all U.S. troops. Once a pariah as the nation's best-known draft dodger, Ali was now seen by many as a symbolic victim of a nation's past sins, even if a large sector still would have liked him locked away. Despite earlier warnings by the FBI, the Nation of Islam had shown little inclination to attempt to overthrow the U.S. government. Anyway, as a major public figure, Ali had by now practically transcended the sect to which he remained so faithful.

On June 15, the U.S. Supreme Court unexpectedly gave Ali's cause a huge boost by decreeing, in a separate ruling, that conscientious-objector status was allowable on religious grounds alone. This was significant to his case in that prosecutors had already acknowledged the sincerity of his religious beliefs; it was his stance as a pacifist they had attacked, on the basis that Muslims are allowed participation in a holy war. His docket had yet to be heard by the Court, but the case against him was severely weakened.

Seeking to capitalize on the shifting public sentiment toward the ex-champion, Ali's people, led by the crafty Harold Conrad, feverishly sought an acceptable site for a megabucks fight against Frazier. They found one in Georgia, a state without a boxing commission. Their efforts were helped immeasurably by Leroy Johnson, a politically powerful black state senator who pleaded with Atlanta mayor Sam Massell to make history by licensing the bout. Massell became a willing ally, penciling in October 26, over the fruitless last-minute objections of Georgia's notorious segregationist governor Lester Maddox, who would declare the date a statewide "Day of Mourning." "He [Maddox] didn't know what was going on," Conrad would gloat years later. "He thought Ali had been cleared to fight by the [U.S.] Supreme Court."

Upon learning the news, Ali refused to celebrate. "I'll believe I have a fight when I hear the bell," he said warily. As it so happened, the Frazier camp wasn't interested—for now. Amid the mad rush to get Ali back in the ring, Frazier had hardly even been consulted; no contracts existed, there had been no negotiations, nothing. To boot, Frazier already had a commitment for another title fight (against light-heavyweight champion Bob Foster) three weeks following the proposed Atlanta date. So another opponent was quickly substituted: Jerry Quarry, a rugged and respected "white hope" contender from California.

With a noticeable bulge around his midsection, Ali resumed serious training at Dundee's Miami gym in September. An ecstatic Dundee saw little ring rust; within weeks the trainer would gush, "moves like silk, hits like a ton." After one grueling afternoon workout, Ali spoke of his mission to reporters: "All of this leaves no time for poems, jokes, or gimmicks. . . . I'm not fightin' one man, I'm fightin' a lot of men, showin' 'em here is one man they couldn't defeat, couldn't conquer, one they didn't see get big and fat and flat on his back."

Ali's Atlanta return was as much a celebration as it was a prizefight. African-American notables dominated the ringside seats: Sidney Poitier, Diana Ross, Jesse Jackson, Andrew Young, Bill Cosby, Hank Aaron, and Coretta Scott King were among those celebrities contributing to the festive air of black pride. Spotting isolated Caucasian ticketholders, Bundini Brown called them "white buttons on a black silk shirt." Before the fight, Ali had unveiled a childlike drawing of the scene as he imagined it, replete with Lester Maddox running down the aisle yelling, "Stop the fight!" as Quarry lay prone in center ring. When asked for a poem, he offered a terse "Quarry-sorry," adding, "I don't have time for rhyme."

Ali entered the ring accompanied by the ritual idolatrous chanting of his name—the prodigal son had returned. He won the fight on a deep eyebrow cut suffered by Quarry in the third round. As far as how much of the "old" Ali was left, the bout was inconclusive, although fans were delighted to see the trademark shuffle and dance in the first round. Quarry, a slow brawler, managed to tag Ali a few times in the second, a clear indication of Ali's loss of foot speed. Still, it was a winning night and a momentous occasion: Ali was fit, alive, and well; no federal marshals blocked the fight; and closed-circuit sales were brisk across the country. The Frazier fight loomed.

❦ ❦ ❦

"I want Joe Frazier."

Six weeks later, Ali was back in the ring—in New York, of all places. Edwin Dooley, still the boxing commissioner in New York, hardly laid out a welcome mat; he reluctantly licensed Ali to fight Oscar Bonavena in Madison Square Garden when ordered to do so by federal district judge Walter Mansfield (following a suit brought by the NAACP), who labeled the commission's past actions "unreasonable discrimination." Ali confronted a red-faced Dooley at the contract signing: "You took my title away. I'm gonna make you give it back."

Bonavena was a risky choice for Ali's second comeback fight. The awkward Argentinian, whom Ali tagged "Beast," had gone twenty-five rounds with Joe Frazier (and knocked him down twice) and had never been KO'd. Not one of Ali's better outings, the fight ended dramatically when the ex-champ floored his stubborn opponent three times in the fifteenth round. Frazier, who had earlier claimed Bonavena couldn't hit Ali with a gun now felt there was no way he could lose to Ali. Screamed Ali after the fight, "I want Joe Frazier!"

The 1971 meeting between Ali and Joe Frazier was initially simply billed "The Fight." Over the years it would come to be known as "The Fight of the Century," but at the time of signing, hype was almost superfluous, since promoters were dealing

JOE FRAZIER

Born in a one-room shack, the son of a one-armed South Carolina tenant farmer, Joe Frazier parlayed Olympic gold, a hammer of a left hand, and a bit of good fortune into a championship career. During his brief prime, he was considered the equal of eminent past heavyweights. Yet he will always be primarily remembered, however unfairly, as Muhammad Ali's greatest opponent.

Frazier proved lucky enough to be in the right place twice in his career and good enough to capitalize on it both times. The first occasion was when Buster Mathis, who'd defeated Frazier in the 1964 Olympic trials, broke his hand. Frazier left his slaughterhouse job, replaced Mathis, and won a gold medal while himself competing with a broken thumb. As with Ali in 1960, the medal led to the requisite career-starting support of a sponsorship group (Cloverlay of Philadelphia). Frazier's second slice of providence turned out to be Ali's exile, which left a heavyweight vacuum. Again, Frazier seized the day by defeating first Buster Mathis, then Jimmy Ellis in separate title bouts.

If Frazier's career was relatively short—thirty-two won (twenty-seven KO's), four lost, one draw—blame his straight-ahead, mule-train attack. As the quintessential boxing gladiator, Frazier took tremendous punishment by dint of his unwavering, punch-absorbing style. The three fights with Ali were wars, two of which resulted in brief hospital stays for Frazier. He was a proud, hardworking athlete who could never accept the humiliation Ali repeatedly heaped on him outside the ring. Once, the two engaged in a very real television studio brawl, a skirmish prompted by an insult from Ali ("You're ignorant, Joe"). Two decades after they first fought, Frazier hadn't mellowed one bit. "I hated Ali," he told Thomas Hauser. "... I'd like to fight Ali-Clay-whatever-his-name-is again tomorrow. Twenty years I've been fighting Ali, and I still want to take him apart piece by piece and send him back to Jesus."

with the most eagerly anticipated sporting event in memory. The battle was set for March 8, with the two participants earning $2.5 million apiece—an unheard-of sum for that period. The combined purse would ultimately escalate the pay scale for major prizefights, but the megadollars for Ali-Frazier paled in significance next to the actual event.

Beneath the large grudge factor at stake between the two participants lay obvious social divisions. The conservative interests favored Frazier, the hardworking, well-muscled brawler with an aggressive and honest style. His partisans made him the blue-collar good guy, a churchgoer whose job it was to shut up for good the draft-dodging Black Muslim. Ali remained an enigma—part con man, part knight-errant returning for revenge. To back him, felt many who did, meant backing individualism and personal freedom, as opposed to promoting the repressive forces of law and order if you liked Joe. Passions everywhere ran deep, and Ali played it to the hilt, calling Frazier a "white hope" and the "Gorilla" and accusing any blacks who favored him of being "Uncle Toms."

Frazier resented Ali's television appearances, his media manipulation, and the manner in which he, Frazier, had been overlooked as champion (even his autobiography was subtitled *The Champ Nobody Knew*). Most of all, he despised how Ali had managed to separate him from the black community. He trained relentlessly in relative obscurity, while Ali fiddled lightheartedly at his festive Miami camp, insisting that Frazier was no threat, dubbing the contest "the champ [himself] and the tramp." One of Ali's favorite refrains promised that if he lost, he would crawl to Frazier, kiss his shoes, and hand over the title of The Greatest.

Before the most electrified, celebrity-studded audience Madison Square Garden had ever seen, the bout began in classic slugger-boxer confrontation. For the first two rounds, Ali jabbed and spun away from Frazier's roundhouse attack, calling to mind his prefight augury: "Joe's gonna come out smokin' . . . and I'll be peckin' and a-pokin.'" But the third round signaled a distinct change in the tenor of the fight. Frazier kept boring in and from that point on, Ali found it surmountingly difficult to fend off his irrepressible opponent. At times he fought brilliantly, albeit unwisely, opting to hook with a hooker, to slug with Frazier for the duration, and it almost worked.

But Frazier was too much the warrior to be swayed by Ali's ring con—the jibes and head pats, the your-punches-don't-hurt headshakes (Frazier knew well they did), the playing to the press ("Nooooo contest," he would yell over the ropes) and the audience. And all too often Ali's legs simply weren't up to whisking him away in time. He absorbed punishment as he never had before; arm-weary and exhausted, he was severely wobbled in the eleventh. In the fifteenth, Frazier dropped the challenger with a pulverizing left hook flush to the jaw. That Ali was at that point able to rise, to halfway recover and resume, revealed remarkable heart and stamina. ("The way they were hitting," offered referee Arthur Mercante afterward, "I was surprised that it went fifteen. They threw some of the best punches I've ever seen.") But in a relatively close fight, the devastating knockdown effectively sealed the decision for Frazier, who remained undefeated. As Bundini Brown would recall, "That punch blew out all the candles on the cake."

"Clay is good," Frazier had said before the fight, "but he isn't good enough to escape." What Frazier hadn't expected was that Ali wouldn't try to escape, that he would fight on the ropes and inside, where his reach advantage would be less effective. "I want them to remember my art and science," Ali had said earlier, but he had shown precious little of both in an otherwise courageous effort. At the evening's end, one reporter suggested to the swollen-cheeked Ali that Frazier thought that he [Ali] would never want to fight him again. "Oh, how wrong he is," said Ali.

The next day, at a press conference, Ali was subdued and self-assured in defeat, correcting well-wishers who addressed him as champ—"Joe's the champ now"—and letting all present know that life goes on. "Just lost a fight, that's all," he shrugged. "Probably be a better man for it. You'll all be writing about something else soon. I had my day. You lose, you don't shoot yourself."

Both men gained from the epic meeting. Frazier, hospitalized from internal injuries, had proven his mettle as champion; Ali, his courage as a warrior. The stage was set for future encounters, even as some of Ali's critics rejoiced in his loss. "If they fought a dozen times," wrote Red Smith, "Joe Frazier would whip Muhammad Ali a dozen times; and it would get easier as they went along."

And oh, how wrong he was.

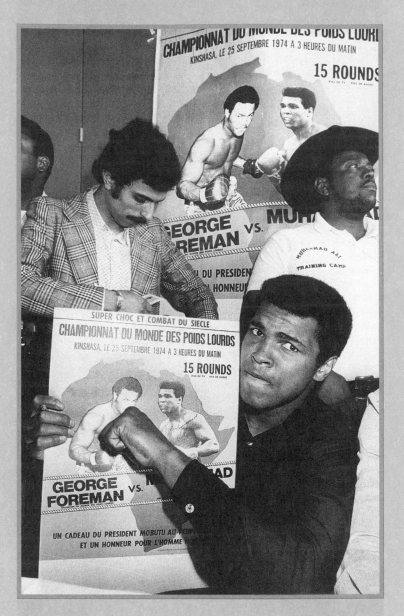

October 1974

THE GREATEST

———◆———

A li never did crawl across the ring in defeat, as promised, to kiss Frazier's feet. Nor did he go into hiding, as Floyd Patterson before him, nor cry over the outcome. If anything, he proved himself more human in defeat than he ever had in victory. The various setbacks he had suffered over the previous few years had provided ample preparation.

Not that he enjoyed his new position. Before the loss to Frazier, he still considered himself the rightful champion. Now, for the first time in seven years, he faced the reality of living without a title that had been legitimately lost. "When I beat Sonny Liston," he told biographer Thomas Hauser, "I was too young to appreciate what I'd done. But when I lost to Frazier, I would have done anything except go against the will of Allah to get my title back again."

A little over a month after Ali's most devastating loss inside the ring, he would enjoy his greatest victory outside it. On April 17, the U.S. Supreme Court declared in a unanimous decision that all charges against Muhammad Ali be dismissed. It was not as clear a ruling as met the eye. The Court had initially been deadlocked at 4–4 (with Thurgood Marshall recusing himself), which would have meant that the lower court's conviction had to stand. But the vote was changed in Ali's favor after Justice Potter Stewart presented a compromise argument whose wording was at once able to reveal flaws in the draft appeal board's earlier ruling without at the same time paving the way for Muslims or other religious objectors to randomly avoid the draft in the future.

Ali was in Chicago preparing for an upcoming bout with Jimmy Ellis when he was stunned by the news. "It's like a man's been in chains all his life, and suddenly the chains are taken off," he told *Sports Illustrated*. "He don't realize he's free until he gets the circulation back in his arms and legs and starts to move his fingers."

Ali wasted little time in resuming his quest to regain the title. He knew that simple economics dictated an eventual rematch with Frazier (there was talk of $3 million for each fighter); the question was simply where and when. In the meantime he would put his considerable earning powers to work by fighting an array of contenders both at home and abroad. His childhood friend from Louisville Jimmy Ellis was a safe first choice.

Having long fought in Ali's shadow, Ellis, who had once bested Ali as an amateur, relished the match. He felt he "knew" Ali in and out from their having sparred thousands of rounds in the past, but the reverse also held true. The recently deposed WBA champion could hardly surprise Ali with anything new, not even with Angelo Dundee in his corner. (Dundee had trained/managed Ellis during Ali's absence; since he was earning more percentagewise on the other side, he had Ali's blessing to stay with Ellis for this one fight.)

It made little difference. Ali's wicked right hand, most effective when following his jab, had become a powerful weapon; in the fourth round in Houston it effectively ended all hope for Ellis. Ali tacked on eight brilliant "stick and move" rounds before the ref stopped the fight with Ellis slumped on the ropes in the twelfth.

After breezing through Ellis, Ali took on blubbery Buster Mathis—the first fight of a new extension contract (four years) with Herbert Muhammad. Following the loss to Frazier, Ali would earn more than $2 million in six fights spread over a year. This was considered a ton of money back then, especially when assessing the workload—an itinerary at the time likened to Joe Louis's "Bum of the Month" club from decades earlier. (Not exactly a fair comparison, since Ali's opponents over his career collectively help make up the most attractive period in heavyweight history.)

Against Mathis and Ellis, Ali was in both instances faulted for "coasting"—ironic, considering the charges of cruelty some years back against Patterson and Terrell. Critics claimed that in these two latest bouts Ali engaged in light sparring when it should have been lights out ("Take him out, damn it, Ali!" screamed Dundee toward the end of the Mathis fight.) Many felt that Ali could have put Mathis down at any time, which he actually did—albeit from the featheriest of punches—in the twelfth round. "How am I goin' to sleep," Ali asked reporters afterward, "if I just killed a man in front of his wife and son just to satisfy you writers?" When a scribe brought up Ali's treatment of Terrell and Patterson, the former champion said, "Them was the days of the draft thing and the religion thing and black against white, all that. Now them days have gone forever. I don't need to do like I did then. I'm more educated and civilized."

Hardly five weeks after his waltz with Mathis, Ali traveled to Switzerland, where he regained knockout form against Jurgen Blin, a no-better-than-average German fighter. The December 26 mismatch ended for the wobbly ex-butcher in the seventh, when his seconds wisely threw in the towel before Ali could do any more damage. "It would have been easier for him to have been knocked out cold," Ali opined afterward.

Following a visit to Saudi Arabia, Ali returned Stateside, where he was himself coldcocked by ex-wife Sonji, who on March 2 obtained a court order in Chicago for $44,000 in back alimony. The money was paid up and just as quickly replaced, thanks to a comfortable spring payday in Tokyo with Mac Foster, another of Ali's former sparring partners.

Ali highly enjoyed the 1972 sojourn to Tokyo; he was treated like visiting royalty and responded with as much of the old-style ham as he could muster. He refereed junior boxing matches, prayed in a temple, visited U.S. airmen at a military base, and jabbered away at training sessions, all to the delight of his hosts. On April Fools' Day he entered the ring in a magnificent silk kimono carrying a huge sign on a tall pole that indicated round five as his knockout prediction. Foster, however, chose a troublesome, hell-bent-on-survival defensive mode that allowed him to outlast the forecast fifth. After that, Ali seemed to lose interest as he ho-hummed his way to a fifteen-round decision. Late in the fight, disgruntled fans yelled, *"Shinken ni yare!"* (We want some serious fighting!)

Next up was a rematch with aging Canadian bruiser George Chuvalo. Set for but one month after his bout with Mac Foster, the bout was regarded as little more than a sweat-breaker for Ali, yet once again, he had to go the distance to defeat a boxer regarded as little more than a human punching bag, a man who two years earlier had been destroyed in but three rounds by rising sensation George Foreman.

Six weeks later, Foreman himself was ringside in Las Vegas for Ali's rematch with Jerry Quarry, a fight ending in a repeat TKO (seventh round). "Ain't this an easy way to make a livin'?" barked Ali at the press row after the fourth round. Quarry was reeling from two savage uppercuts when Ali ("I didn't want to kill nobody") waved in referee Mike Kaplan for the stoppage. Afterward, Foreman indulged Ali in some obligatory I-want-you, let's-go-right-now woofing. Few present could have possibly imagined that such ritual theatrics would ultimately lead to a fight for the ages.

In August 1972 Hollywood called on Ali with a heady offer to star in a remake of *Here Comes Mr. Jordan*, with a script written by Francis Ford Coppola. The money was fabulous, Ali was definitely interested, but the project was scotched by Elijah Muhammad. The plot, involving an athlete's reincarnation, was unacceptable to Elijah. So Ali had to pass, for now, on an even easier way to make a living.

❧   ❧   ❧

"I'll just go on makin' money . . ."

Ali continued to weave his way through the year with a succession of wins over less-than-testing opponents. To his management's credit, each outing had its own built-in angle, however stretched. In Dublin, against Al "Blue" Lewis, a return to boxing's home turf was touted as the first major heavyweight

◆ DEER LAKE ◆

Midway through 1972, Muhammad Ali realized a career-long desire when he purchased a hilly tract of wooded land in Deer Lake, Pennsylvania, where he built a year-round training camp. At the center, he constructed a standard boxing gym around which were scattered log cabins, a mess hall, a barn, and outbuildings. Spread around the property were huge boulders upon which Cassius Clay, Sr., had painted names of famous fighters—an impression Ali had retained from his brief stay at Archie Moore's camp.

Ali loved his spartan hideaway, which, however secluded, was always open to visitors. The place also served as a home to various members of the entourage. Many cast members would come and go, but regulars such as cook Lana Shabazz, helpers Ralph Thornton and Booker Johnson, and unofficial camp manager Gene Kilroy (who first spotted the location), were reliably on hand for the weeks that led up to Ali's fights in the 1970s.

For Ali, the camp allowed him to focus on boxing and at the same time enjoy a new, self-created role as country squire to his helpers and hangers-on. Prior to the purchase of Deer Lake, the humdrum of training had grown old, leaving him depressed and often unprepared. No longer. Ali himself called his camp "a valid place for fighters to come and work and sweat like fighters should, not like all those places with chandeliers and thick carpets and all those pretty girls around."

TRAINING AT DEER LAKE.

fight in Ireland in sixty-four years; at Madison Square Garden in November, it was a heralded rerun with Floyd Patterson (who wound up too bloodied to answer the eighth-round bell); in Stateline, Nevada, it was the alleged speed of light-heavyweight champion Bob Foster, who, perhaps because he was outweighed by forty pounds, managed to get knocked down seven times. (Foster's most lasting contribution to Ali's record was that of being the first opponent to draw blood—a five-stitch cut over the eye.) This last fight seemed to depress Ali, who afterward called it "just another night to jump up and down and beat up somebody." Where was Frazier?

All the while that Ali was padding his bankroll and staying fit by fighting all comers (well, almost), Joe Frazier was woefully inactive. The new champion spent considerable time recovering from the physical aftereffects of his win over Ali, touring Europe with his lounge band. When he finally did return it was only to fight two pathetically inadequate challengers, Ron Stander and Terry Daniels, ten and fifteen months later, respectively. Despite some highly attractive purse offerings, he seemed in no hurry for a rematch with Ali. So it was that he ill-advisedly took on George Foreman in what would amount to a flat-out, career-ruining train wreck.

In the long run, Frazier's January 22, 1973, loss to Foreman—a devastating second-round, six-knockdown affair in which Frazier was visibly lifted off the floor by a Foreman blow to the temple—held mixed blessings for Ali. "My, there goes $5 million out the window," he reportedly said when learning the result. Gone was Frazier's undefeated record, and, in turn, his status as a drawing card. Yet here was a new champion, another sullen, hard-punching "villain" on which Ali could feast his sights and unleash his psychological wrath. There were now two dragons in the picture.

A few weeks after Frazier's demise, Ali was back in Vegas to take on Joe Bugner, the latest British hope. Ali entered the ring in a dazzling, bejeweled robe—a gift from Elvis, one of his heroes. He cut Bugner early, then spent twelve fruitless rounds trying to put the foreigner away. After Ali had earned another clear-cut, relatively monotonous decision, some observers talked openly about the now thirty-one-year-old's waning skills; others felt that Ali had simply overtrained, what with sixty-seven rounds of sparring the week before. Afterward, Ali focused right in on Foreman: "He's not going to get near me now, but that's all right. I don't need him. I'm in a world of my own. Why should I fret? I'll just go on makin' money—like a couple of million in the next couple of years." Some cynics felt the entire performance was but a well-laid trap, designed to entice the new champion.

But that was before the debacle in San Diego, the incomprehensible loss two months later to then unknown Ken Norton—a man who had earned but a piddly $300 in his previous fight. Thought of as just another payday ($275,000) opponent, the deceptively eighth-ranked Norton broke Ali's jaw with a grazing blow in the second round. The "lucky" punch happened to catch Ali with his mouth open, fracturing the mandible exactly at a point where he was missing a back tooth. Adding proverbial insult to injury, Norton took the verbal offensive as well, repeatedly braying, "You're nothing," as he dominated the middle rounds. With Ali covering up in excruciating pain, the muscled ex-Marine was able to effectively hammer home a crude yet close decision. As against Frazier, Ali lost the fight but gained untold respect for the courage to continue a fight that by all rights should have been stopped. "Winning took priority over proper medical care," recalled Ali's doctor, Ferdie Pacheco. "It's sick."

Ali would later offer a bizarre excuse, something about his taking a running swing at a golf ball three weeks earlier—"revolutionizin' the game," he called it—a stunt that earned him a three-hundred-yard drive as well as a sorely twisted ankle that limited training. Such an injury would have meant postponement against the likes of Frazier, or even Patterson or Quarry, but why blow the dough against a no-threat? "When I'm ready I'll take this guy back," snorted Ali postfight, refusing to acknowledge Norton by name. But in the meantime, the plans for megabuck title bouts were suddenly in shambles. Even the usually voluble Howard Cosell was at a loss for words, muttering, "I just don't understand."

❧ ❧ ❧

"... a better Ali."

Despite a career that was once again ostensibly in ruins, the very-former champion confidently announced his plans through clenched teeth (and a wired jaw) at a press conference two weeks later: Knock out first Ken Norton, then Joe Frazier, and finally George Foreman—all within the next two years. "Took a broken jaw to let me stay home and enjoy my wife and children," he shrugged before vowing to resume serious roadwork in three weeks. "When I come back, people are going to see a better Ali."

True to his agenda, Ali scheduled Norton as the first order of redemption. "I took a nobody and created a monster," he moaned (jaw now healed) before the September 1973 return bout in Los Angeles. "I put him on 'The Dating Game.'" There was no small interest in the rematch, most of it fueled not by what a force Norton might be but by whether Ali was washed up. For all his herculean strength, Norton was never a great fighter. His chin-down, two-step, stop-and-punch style, however, proved terribly difficult for Ali to get around. Ali did prevail in the sequel, but only after standing dead center ring and slugging his way to a winning final round, which turned out to be the difference in the fight. Visibly miffed over what had amounted to an even showdown, Ali took a swing at his sidekick Bundini after the final bell. The frustrations of such a close fight didn't sit well. Ego aside, Ali the businessman knew that purse offerings down the road relied on his performance.

By the end of 1973 the heavyweight scene was very much up in the air. No one, save Ali, really wanted Foreman; Frazier

Ali squeaked out a decision against Ken Norton in Ali-Norton III, 1976.

had become a spectacular mystery; and Ali's stock seemed in rapid free fall following the double dose of Norton. Yet to no one's surprise, the show still revolved around Ali; whatever his physical limitations, the mouth still roared.

That Ali exhibited obvious flaws in the Norton fights, that Frazier was now a question mark after the thrashing by Foreman, mattered little to the twenty thousand who would throng Madison Square Garden for the long-awaited rematch in February 1974. Ali's promotional wizardry had once again set the table for a nasty grudge match, even if it was being held at least a year too late. His childish verbal attacks ("Joe Frazier's sooo ugly," etc.) stoked Frazier's hatred, a loathing that ran as deep as Ali's thirst for revenge. For their bout-jeopardizing TV studio fracas five days before the event, the two were docked $5,000 each by the Boxing Commission—an insignificant sum considering their nearly $2 million in guarantees and the ticket sales the tiff would generate.

Matching the fevered pitch of their first battle was next to impossible, and in this sense, Ali-Frazier II was anticlimactic. Otherwise it was a good, near-great fight, once again dictated by contrasting styles, each superb in its own right. In the end it was Ali, the ring general, whose jab measured up to his jabber, over Frazier, the relentless foot soldier. Only in the middle rounds did Joe's smoke make any difference, but even then, once Ali dug in and squared off, the power punch exchanges were remarkably even. Frazier claimed later that he'd been robbed, but if referee Tony Perez hadn't controversially rushed in to protect him from an Ali onslaught in the second round—Perez thought he'd heard the bell—the fight might have been over right then. In his dressing room, an unmarked Ali mugged for the press. "Can you believe," he asked, "that this is the face of a thirty-two-year-old man who has just fought Joe Frazier twelve rounds?"

"A-li, booma-ya!"

The 1974 win over Frazier may have brought Ali sweet revenge (along with more than $1 million), but it hardly reestablished him as the force he had once been. And when, seven weeks later, George Foreman knocked Ken Norton halfway across a Venezuelan boxing ring, many Ali fans feared for the ex-champ's ultimate safety. Going by past performance, how could Ali even think of challenging a slugger who had so casually destroyed Ali's two greatest nemeses in two rounds each? But by now, the boxing world had to know that Ali thrived on challenge, and that he lived for the shot to vault back to center stage, where he would at least be sure to dominate until actual fight time.

And center stage this time clearly involved the entire world. The event was arranged for Kinshasa, Zaire, in the heart of darkest Africa, thanks largely to the machinations of Don King, who stressed the concept of a championship fight between blacks, promoted by a black man, in a country ruled by blacks. Through a series of intermediaries, King was able to secure the approval and necessary financing from Zaire's ruling strongman, Mobutu Sese Seko, who saw the fight as a vehicle to lure foreign investors; in turn, the two principals were themselves drawn by then stratospheric offers of $5 million each. Thanks primarily to Ali's status as international icon, this boxing match, scheduled for September 25, was a good bet to reach an unprecedented level of worldwide attention.

For Ali, the setting for his latest epiphany could not have been more perfect. Just before Frazier II, he had beaten Dutchman Rudi Lubbers in Indonesia and reveled in the adulation of

GEORGE FOREMAN

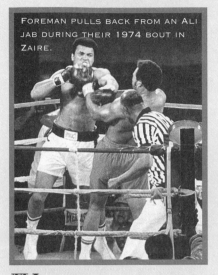

FOREMAN PULLS BACK FROM AN ALI JAB DURING THEIR 1974 BOUT IN ZAIRE.

When informed that the fight in Zaire would take place in the wee hours of the morning, George Foreman said that was fine, that he'd "had a lot of fights at three or four in the morning." Like many champions past, Foreman was a child of the ghetto, in this case Houston's Fifth Ward. His checkered adolescence included vandalism and mugging winos for cheap booze. His days as a street bully ended when he joined the Job Corps, where he was ultimately persuaded by a vocational counselor to take up boxing.

In Mexico City in 1968, Foreman made headlines first by winning a gold medal (over Soviet favorite Ionas Chapulis) and then by holding up two tiny American flags during his victory ceremony. Days earlier, track stars Tommy Smith and Carlos Williams had been suspended after raising clenched fists on their dais to celebrate black power. Foreman's gesture was seen at the time as an affront to African-American solidarity, as well as a slap at Muhammad Ali, whose allegedly unpatriotic stance had resulted in boxing exile. (Before traveling to Zaire, Ali had attended the annual Boxing Writers' Dinner, where he screamed at Foreman, "I'm gonna beat your Christian ass, you white, flag-waving bitch, you!" Later he added, "I can't let him win. He represents pork chops.")

Back in his prime, Foreman never had many fans, not even when he took on five different boxers consecutively in one silly telecast event six months after Zaire. He retired in 1977, only to make a remarkable comeback ten years later. What's more, he had by then somehow transformed himself into a warm and roly-poly, country-preaching (he had become a minister) pitchman who had little trouble winning over a previously diffident sporting public. He further shocked the boxing world by knocking out Michael Moorer for the WBA title at age forty-five on November 5, 1994.

thirty-five thousand fans. "Places we go that you would think people never heard of him, they heard of him," said Angelo Dundee. In Zaire, training at a remote jungle compound, Ali took up a predictable battle cry: "This is my country." His voluble promotional drumbeat thumped to often insensitive extremes, even as he praised his hosts. In one breath he would ramble on about the wonder of black doctors, black pilots, black heads of state; in another he would threaten Foreman that his "African friends" would put him in a pot. He latched on to a few phrases of the regional native tongue, most memorably a rallying cheer that, sounded by locals, would haunt his dour opponent right up to the opening bell: "A-li, booma-ya! A-li, booma-ya!" (Ali, kill him!)

While Ali mingled and joked as he trained, Foreman had a lousy time of it. The champion would only venture out of his hillside quarters to walk his German shepherd, Daggo, a police dog seen by natives as a symbol of colonial rule. A rumor among Zairians that Foreman was actually a black Belgian had local *feticheurs* (witch doctors) swamped with requests to fix the fight against him. The cranky Foreman offered occasional snippets such as "I don't like fights—I just land the right punch and everything is over" and "My opponents don't worry about losing, they worry about getting hurt." Otherwise, he stayed in seclusion behind armed guards.

Eight days before the appointed hour—4:00 A.M., for live showing in the States—Foreman suffered a nasty cut over the right eye while sparring. The bout was temporarily off as all parties scrambled for cover. Rumors flew—both fighters were said to be skipping town—and the promoters and the Zairian authorities were up in arms. The fight was quickly rescheduled for October 30, providing Ali with countless more occasions for joyous hype, and Foreman with another stir-crazy month in which to brood. Both parties were asked (warned) by the government not to leave the country.

When the big day finally arrived, the betting odds ran three to one against Ali. As with the Liston fight ten years earlier, boxing scribes predicted a massacre. Surely the challenger would do his best to dance out of harm's way for as long as possible, but consensus had it that the champion would at some point connect. Even Ali's seconds were very concerned for his survival. In the dressing room at the stadium, it remained for Ali to reassure them. "This ain't nothing but another day in the dramatic life of Muhammad Ali," he shrugged. "Do I look scared? I fear Allah and thunderstorms and bad plane rides, but this is like another day in the gym."

In Thomas Hauser's *Muhammad Ali,* reporter Jack Newfield lists Ali's variety of identities as "manchild, con man, entertainer, poet, draft dodger, rebel, evangelist, champion." On the fabled night in Zaire the con man made an early appearance, only to be relieved by the champion at the finish. No one, least of all Foreman, could ever have predicted the wild, wigged-out manner by which this bout, entirely orchestrated by Ali, would proceed.

To begin with, Ali, rather than dance away, startled Foreman at the opening bell with a couple of quick shots in close. Some thirty seconds later he retreated into the ropes, as if welcoming Foreman to whale away at will. Foreman, expecting a long, tiring chase of a fight, was only too happy to oblige. Ali's corner screamed for their charge to move away and box, but he refused. Foreman's bombs were fraught with danger, but Ali's guile and contortions kept them from connecting. Just before the bell, Ali let loose with a neat flurry of lefts and rights to further confuse matters. Welcome to the "rope-a-dope"—the latest installment of resident boxing genius.

◆ NICKNAMES ◆

A RARE FRIENDLY ENCOUNTER WITH JOE FRAZIER.

As part of his prefight intimidation routine, Ali was fond of tagging opponents with unflattering nicknames. Most were clever free associations based either on the physical appearances or the fight styles of adversaries.

Ali himself earned a number of monickers in his early days as a pro, among them Cash the Brash, Gaseous Cassius, The Mighty Mouth, The Kentucky Rooster, and, most notably, The Louisville Lip.

Some of the more memorable:

Cleveland Williams	The Pussycat
Floyd Patterson	The Rabbit
Joe Frazier	The Gorilla
George Chuvalo	The Washerwoman
George Foreman	The Mummy
Sonny Liston	The Bear
Charlie Powell	The Beast
Larry Holmes	The Peanut
Earnie Shavers	The Acorn

For the next few rounds the pattern continued: Ali, planted on the ropes, riding out the heavy blows to the body, ducking others, and landing with his own combos each time Foreman paused. Midway through the third, Foreman's power was ever slightly beginning to wane, and Ali let him know it: "C'mon, champ, you can do better than that. . . . Show me something, George." And as Foreman's punches grew slower and less threatening, as the champion became more and more exhausted, so, too, was it easier for Ali to counter. The challenger was living up to a prefight vow to be "the Mummy's Curse."

By the fifth, Ali's strategy was finally clear to all ("giving him a lot of nothing," Dundee would call it). He continued to lie and sway over the top rope, but now buoyed with success, he covered up less and talked more. "Punch, sucker. That's a sissy punch," and finally, "Now it's my turn." And so it was. In the sixth and seventh rounds Ali peppered away as the drained Foreman lunged wildly, falling into Ali's arms with every wasted effort. Finally, in the eighth, two right hands and a left hook, followed by a chopping right, toppled Foreman. He struggled groggily to get up and nearly made it, but the fight was over. Ali had won back his title.

On the way back from the stadium to his quarters on the Zaire River, Ali's convoy moved through a torrential downpour as people lined the roads. Word of the conquest had traveled from village to village, and now people cheered in the rain at the mere glimpse of the champion's car. Three hours later, Ali was up talking to the press, expounding on retiring, on working for Allah, and on his role as the most well-known person on earth. But just as quickly, he was back with a rhetorical question: "Don't I look like I've got a few more years left?"

May 1977

CHAPTER SEVEN

LATE ROUNDS

Ali's monumental victory in Africa was received with joy the world over. As shocking as it was, the result saw a natural order returned to sport, a result that vindicated the wrongs long suffered by the all-hailed conquering hero. The shock of the upset quickly wore off, and Ali just as quickly grasped the official mantle of ring royalty that he'd always considered his due.

Ali had long enjoyed the attention of kings and heads of state; his stature as an international figure transcended the athletic abilities that lay behind it. But after Zaire, Ali seemed to give of himself more and more in public. Championship belts aside, he was now, more than ever, a man of the people, a champ who relished every moment of recognition the title brought him. He kissed babies in the street, he posed for photos, he visited hospitals, prisons, and schools. A biographer once wrote that it had to be Ali's "secret wish to be seen by every man, woman, and child on planet earth." "I'm like a little ant," Ali would say. "Lots of other little ants know me, follow me. So God gives me some extra power."

Ali won a number of awards following the title win in late 1974: *Ring Magazine*'s Fighter of the Year, *Sports Illustrated*'s Sportsman of the Year, and the Hickock Award to the top professional athlete. There were ceremonies in Chicago and New York, a parade in Louisville, and most amazingly, a visit to the White House. Barely three years removed from the threat of a prison sentence, here was Ali being invited by President Gerald Ford, as part of an effort to heal past wounds. "You made a big mistake letting me come," quipped Ali upon meeting the president, "because now I'm going after your job."

Through all the upheaval in Ali's life, in his role as celebrity and champion, there remained one constant: his devotion to the Nation of Islam and the teachings of Elijah Muhammad. Yet even those steadfast beliefs would change with the sudden death of Elijah Muhammad in a Chicago cardiac unit on February 25, 1975. Upon Elijah's passing, his son Wallace Muhammad took over leadership and turned the group toward a less marginalized, more orthodox Islam. Ali followed the new direction of Wallace, which entailed acceptance of all races. "We Muslims hate injustice and evil," said Ali at the time, "but we don't have time to hate people. White people wouldn't be here if God didn't mean them to be."

As the once and present champion, Ali reiterated his vow to fight all comers, his refusal to duck anyone. His first title defense, against Chuck Wepner, a.k.a. "The Bayonne Bleeder," is today best remembered as the inspiration behind the Rocky movies. Billed as the "chance of a lifetime" (Wepner's, that is), Ali's messy March 1975 matchup with the unranked, brawling liquor salesman was attended by then unemployed actor

Sylvester Stallone, who saw the germ of a screen idea in the contest between blue-collar underdog and polished champ.

True to his pronounced style, Wepner committed a wealth of fouls in the brutal bout as Ali complained bitterly to referee Tony Perez. (Perez would later file and lose a $20 million lawsuit over Ali's defamatory comments: "He's a dirty ref, a dirty dog.") Predictably, Wepner bled profusely from a cut suffered in the eighth round ("more transfusion than boxing match," one columnist described it), but the fight lugged onward until a furious barrage from Ali left Wepner helpless on the ropes near the end of the fifteenth. One of the evening's few highlights was a knockdown suffered by Ali that he claimed resulted not from a punch but rather from Wepner stepping on his foot and pushing him. (Fifteen years later, at a social gathering, Wepner thought himself unrecognized by Ali, until Ali ambled over and with a wink came down on Wepner's foot.) "I figured I held my own with one of the greatest fighters that ever lived," said a proud Wepner after the fight.

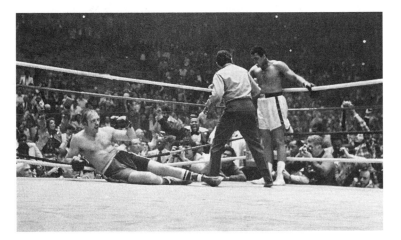

Ali finally puts the real-life "Rocky" Chuck Wepner down for good in the fifteenth round of their 1975 bout.

◆ DON KING ◆

ALI WITH PROMOTER
DON KING, 1977.

Blustery promoter Don King was always known as The Teflon Man, because nothing ever stuck to him—neither grand jury investigations, nor damages sought from lawsuits, nor criminal charges of fraud or tax evasion. Ever since Ali-Foreman, his first major production, the slippery, electric-haired King has been an indomitable force in heavyweight boxing. Without Ali, he might never have made it.

Fresh out of jail for manslaughter, King broke into boxing in 1972 by courting Ali's pro bono services for a charity benefit for a Cleveland hospital. The event netted $10,000 for the hospital, $30,000 for King. He then scrambled up the professional ranks by riding the coattails of Ali, Frazier, and Foreman, securing their allegiance by pushing black unity. He eventually gained a stranglehold on heavyweights (and other divisions) by having his boxers sign exclusive contracts granting him multiple options. (Thanks to Muslim guidance, Ali avoided

King's "exclusives," though he, too, would eventually suffer from the promoter's abuse.) A rival promoter once characterized King as one who "talks black, lives white, and thinks green."

Another promoter tells a story about King's machinations. When Ugandan middleweight prospect John Mugabi won in the first round of a King-promoted fight in Atlantic City in 1982, he made a transatlantic call to Mugabi's English promoter, Mickey Duff, after the fight. "That's one mean mother you got there," King told Duff. "But I was talking with him after the fight, and he said he wants to come with me. I told him that since you and I are friends, I wouldn't take him on unless he cuts you in for fifty percent."

Duff interrupted: "Hold it, Don. I didn't know you spoke Swahili." King confessed that he didn't. "Well, that's interesting," Duff continued, "since Mugabi doesn't speak any English."

Boxing regulations stipulate that you can't both promote and manage a fighter for the obvious conflict of interest. King got around that by having his son Carl act as de facto manager to his promotional charges. That's how nearly every King fighter would eventually wind up on the paper trail of litigants seeking just compensation. And to perpetuate control, King routinely held a piece of both boxers in the ring. "He didn't only cut your end," said '80s champ Larry Holmes, "he made money on you, your opponent, and the networks."

In 1977 King burned the networks with the corrupt U.S. Boxing Championships—a televised (ABC) "tourney" that was revealed to include fixed fights, bribes, and phony rankings. King drew no blame from an investigative committee and was never charged, but neither was anyone else who was involved blamed or charged, although the wrongdoings had been established. He rebounded to promote Ali's penultimate fight against Larry Holmes in 1980, after which he convinced Ali to accept $50,000 cash for $1 million debt. Ali never complained.

In the early '90s, King's viselike grip on boxing was thought to be loosening, what with boxer Mike Tyson in jail for rape. But Tyson, upon his release in 1995, amazed everyone by signing a multimillion-dollar deal with King, the man who'd allegedly left him nearly broke. "Don King has been written off more times than the national debt," once remarked boxing historian Bert Randolph Sugar, one of King's many critics. "It would be foolish ever to count him out."

Despite the event's poor marketability, Muhammad Ali earned a cool $1.5 million. Promoter Don King, who allegedly financed the fight with Cleveland mob money, willingly overpayed Ali in a gamble for the champion's loyalty down the road.

Two months after the Wepner bloodbath, Ali was in Vegas mixing up styles against ex-convict/rugged challenger Ron Lyle. When the rope-a-dope strategy failed to lure Lyle the way it had Foreman, Ali opted to bang flat-footed center ring—to no clear advantage. Behind on points, the champion then took to dancing and jabbing, and in the eleventh caught Lyle with a sudden thunderous right, followed by an uncontested volley that ended the fight. As he had so often done in the past, Ali once again began sluggishly and finished sluggingly. At thirty-three, with his best years behind him, he remained the savviest and often the quickest heavyweight around.

❧ ❧ ❧

"It's real hatred."

In the course of a publicity hunt for a new angle, Ali was persuaded to announce on the eve of his next fight (a June rematch against Joe Bugner in Malaysia) that he was officially retiring. With a $2.2 million purse and the fight in a Muslim country, Ali seemed to be enjoying himself, so the announcement caught many by surprise. Of course, Ali had no intention of quitting the fight game, not with the lucrative rubber match with Frazier on the horizon. Reporters questioning Ali—who easily decisioned Bugner in Kuala Lumpur—had only to mention Frazier by name to get a rise out of the champ: "I want him baaad!"

For Ali, the days leading up to Ali-Frazier III, the October 1975 "Thrilla in Manila," arguably the greatest heavyweight fight of all time, brought on the end of his second marriage. Despite behind-the-scenes talk of his numerous casual encounters, Ali had over the recent past kept up a solemn public display of devotion to Belinda, his Muslim wife. In Manila, however, Ali chose indiscreetly to parade around prefight festivities with California model Veronica Porsche, a woman who'd quietly been his steady companion since Zaire.

Belinda knew of the arrangement, and so would the rest of the world when *Newsweek* ran a story about Veronica passing as Ali's wife at a presidential palace reception hosted by Ferdinand Marcos. (Marcos: "You have a very beautiful wife, Mr. Ali." Ali: "Yours ain't so bad either.") When the piece appeared, Ali was irate over the coverage. "I know celebrities don't have privacy, but at least they should be able to sleep with who they want," he raged at a press conference. "The only person I answer to is Belinda Ali, and I don't worry about her." This last comment made it back Stateside to Belinda, who hopped the next plane to Manila. She stormed into the hotel, fought briefly with her husband behind closed doors, then just as quickly headed back home, their marriage in ruins. People in the Frazier camp relished the chaos, but it was just the sort of thing Ali seemed to thrive on.

As with their previous fight buildups Ali jumped at every chance to berate, belittle, insult, and humble his opponent. "It'll be a thrilla, a killa, a chilla when I get the Gorilla in Manila," Ali would rant over and over, sometimes pummeling a little toy gorilla he kept in his pocket. Though nearly always offended, Frazier remained dead serious as ever, saying things such as, "It's real hatred" and "I want to take his heart out."

Newark Star Ledger reporter Jerry Izenberg said it best when he described Ali-Frazier III as not so much a world title fight as a heavyweight championship of "each other." Few bouts in his-

⬥ ALI'S ENTOURAGE ⬥

ALI WITH THIRD WIFE
VERONICA PORSCHE AND
DAUGHTER HANA, 1977.

WC↑ WC↓ →

By 1974 and the time of Ali-Foreman, Ali's traveling circus had grown to outlandish proportions. Besides Angelo Dundee and assorted close associates, there were any number of characters and hustlers along for the ride, some more legitimate than others. In San Juan, for his first fight after Manila, Ali picked up the tab for fifty-five hotel rooms. Boxing reporters at times tried to place new faces in camp with a game called "What do he do?"

Some among them, like Bundini

Brown, would fall out of favor with the champ, only to jump back on the gravy train. Herbert Muhammad once called the group "a little town" of which Ali was the "mayor, judge, sheriff, and treasurer," adding that Ali "believes in forgiveness. If he stressed justice there wouldn't be anybody around."

The following individuals comprised the inner core, the career-long faithful:

Drew Bundini Brown was Ali's

loudest cheerleader; a kind of court jester who in turn annoyed, amused, and applauded Ali. He came up with Ali's signature "Float like a butterfly, sting like a bee." Bundini died alone in a Los Angeles motel room in the late eighties.

Howard Bingham was Ali's best friend and photographic Boswell. A Hollywood stills photographer by profession, in the course of everyday life with Ali he shot and compiled a staggering catalog of the most photogenic athlete in history.

Dr. Ferdie Pacheco was Ali's longtime personal physician, a man who tried in vain to persuade Ali to retire at the right time. He came to Ali through Dundee, who knew him from Miami where Pacheco often helped Dundee's fighters. Pacheco went on to a career in broadcasting.

Rahaman Ali once sparred with Ali and fought on his undercards; in the later years he was basically brother, companion, and head cheerleader.

Wally Youngblood (Muhammad) was an affable organizer, corner bottle man, and assistant to Dundee.

Gene Kilroy was, other than Dundee and Pacheco, the clan's only white. He was a man without a title, but a great facilitator, advance man, and unofficial camp manager and traveling secretary.

Lloyd Wells, a former pro football player, was another sort of facilitator, a charmer who managed to keep an endless stream of female companionship to a champion's liking.

Lana Shabazz was Ali's personal cook, nutritionist, and surrogate mother at camp. She had cooked for Malcolm X and Elijah Muhammad before leaving a job as a cook at a Muslim restaurant to join Ali. She remained to the end.

Pat Patterson was lent in 1974 by Mayor Richard J. Daley to Ali from the Chicago police force to become Ali's full-time bodyguard in 1974. Patterson had guarded Elijah Muhammad in the sixties. He returned to the beat after Ali retired.

Luis Sarria took daily care of Ali's body as personal masseur. In addition, the quiet, elderly Cuban brought a lifetime of ring knowledge to his exclusive position as Ali's conditioning trainer. Angelo Dundee credits Sarria with giving Ali his excellent physique.

tory have been so truthfully personal, so honestly warlike from start to brutal finish. In the beginning—10:45 A.M. Philippines time for the telecast home—it was Ali, predictably quick from the gate, snapping jabs and spitting epithets, standing fast and rocking blows delivered with every ounce of malevolence he could muster. The early rounds were all his, yet the momentum shifted slightly by the fourth as the snorting Frazier bore in, his lifelong antagonist within hook's reach.

"Stay mean with him, champ!" yelled Ali's seconds, sensing the change. And in the sixth a couple of hooks landed and visibly swiveled Ali's head, punches Frazier would later say "could bring down the walls of a city." Ali may have even visited the "Near Room," his name for the threshold of unconsciousness. And yet he somehow survived the onslaught with that dazed and grim courage that continued to surprise those so used to his glib outer shell. "They told me Joe Frazier was washed up," he mumbled, coming out for the seventh. "They lied," answered Frazier.

By the end of the tenth, the fight was all even as Frazier continued to force the attack. But in the next round Ali, summoning some unfathomable resolve, repelled Frazier with a series of long right hands that connected on the challenger's open face. Gradually their cumulative effect would sap Frazier's strength and drive to the point where Ali regained control. In the thirteenth, he knocked Frazier's mouthpiece out into the crowd. In the fourteenth, one of Frazier's eyes had closed shut; the other was a mere slit. Over Frazier's slurred protests, his wizened trainer, Eddie Futch, threw in the towel. "It's all over," he said. "No one will ever forget what you did here today."

"If God ever calls me to a Holy War," said Ali after the fight, "I want Joe Frazier beside me." But Ali already had his own private Holy War going against the boxing gods who were telling him to surrender. And this was a war he could only fight alone, and with a body never quite the same after the terrible struggle of Manila, a fight he would call "the closest thing to death." Friends urged him to quit, but Ali, with ego and finances never completely in check, kept his circus on the road.

❧ ❧ ❧

"I don't want to look bad."

After five months of recuperation following the Thrilla in Manila, Ali sought a low-risk, million-dollar patsy. He found one in Belgian champion Jean-Pierre Coopman, who, thanks to a little prefight hype, was nicknamed the "Lion of Flanders." Coopman was to go down—and he did, in the fifth round—as one of the most comical of all of Ali's career victims. Ali had serious problems developing animus for a fighter who wanted to kiss him at every press conference.

If Ali had embarked on another bum-of-the-month tour, at least his opponents were allotted their fifteen minutes of fame. Coopman, who drank champagne in his dressing room before the fight, would make a career of public appearances after it, sheerly on the basis of having been in the ring with The Greatest. With some trademark free association, Ali spoke to imagined critics after the fight: "He fell and I felt sorry for him. . . . We live in a freakish world, a vicious world. People like to see blood. . . . People want life and death from me all the time. . . . Let me have a little rest in between."

Angelo Dundee called Jimmy Young, Ali's next opponent, "a boxer, a cute fighter—not great, but a threat." In Landover on April 30, 1976, Young proved much too cute for comfort. In the process, he made Ali, who escaped with a controversial fifteen-round decision, look like a washed-up palooka. The terribly out-of-shape Ali was saved principally by the age-old scoring notion that a fighter's belt must be "taken" from him in aggressive fashion for a challenger to win on points. Young fought defensively—passively, even—with a style that perplexed Ali, who pushed and pulled his lighter opponent as many in the crowd of 12,500 booed heartily. "The worst fight of his career," Dundee called it.

Less than a month later, Ali was in Munich fighting Richard Dunn, an unskilled British opponent who would hit the canvas five times before getting KO'd in the fifth. In so doing, Dunn indirectly helped restore some of Ali's lost luster. (How could anyone know that these would be the last knockdowns of Ali's career?) "I don't want to look bad," Ali had said beforehand. "I let the public down last time." Before the fight, Ali had cut his purse by $100,000 in exchange for some 2,000 tickets comped to American military personnel. "I didn't go [in the army] because of my religion," he told writer Mike Katz, "but them soldiers are just doing their job."

In Munich in his hotel suite, Ali blew up at various members of his entourage for years of indiscriminate charging. "I feed you niggers," he raged. "I take you all over the world and you treat me like this. Nobody has this kind of crowd around him, not even Frank Sinatra."

Having padded his bankroll with the three previous soft touches (and one silly exhibition), Ali again prepared for another major career-testing battle, against the troublesome Ken Norton. He would need the money. Four weeks before their September '76 Yankee Stadium rubber match, Ali's training was interrupted by his wife's filing of divorce papers that charged him with desertion, adultery, and mental cruelty. Ali was at the time contentedly ensconced with Veronica, and Belinda, the faithfully tolerant

Muslim wife and mother of Ali's four children, had had enough. Four months later, the divorce would be made official with a settlement to Belinda that included $670,000, a house in Chicago, and $1 million trust fund for the children. A few years earlier, Ali's parents had themselves separated, due in large part to the father's own womanizing.

Since only one point separated Norton and Ali on the judges' cards of their two previous decisions, their third match figured to be a close one. For all the difficulty Ali had trying to handle Norton's awkward style in the ring, he'd been relatively civil to the challenger outside it. This changed abruptly at a prefight medical exam, when Ali called Norton a "yellow nigger" and a "disgrace to your race" for having appeared in what Ali considered a racially exploitative film. Ali's staged act was thought to be as much about selling tickets as it was a vulgar way to pump himself up.

Norton-Ali III began, like the previous two, with the suggestion that Ali was in effect finished as a fighter. With meager talents, Norton won the majority of the early rounds, essentially by willing his uninspiring style over Ali, while the champion taunted, clowned, and mugged to the crowd. Ali had trained himself into top condition, yet gone with age were the jabs, the combinations, and any semblance of ring movement. But then in the mid to late rounds, Norton seemed to unravel mentally as he tried to pace himself, at one point foolishly parodying Ali by hanging on to the ropes. Meanwhile, Ali, without landing hard punches, managed to look like he'd taken control. Always a master of the clinch, he used the tactic to frustrate and exhaust the muscled Norton. The fight was dead even going into the final round, when Norton's cornermen gave him the bone-headed advice to keep out of trouble. Ali escaped with a whisker-thin split decision.

There was a great deal of postfight sentiment that Norton had been "jobbed." One scribe would later write that he hadn't lost as much as he'd been "snubbed," owing to the Ali mystique. After the fight, Ali faced a hostile press corps. He snapped when a large black reporter asked him, "How long do you intend to fight with your mouth?" Answer: "Long enough to whup your black ass."

Before the press had entered the dressing room, Ali had confided in Ferdie Pacheco that maybe it was "time to call it quits. If I can't beat Norton . . . I've got to get out of this before I start getting hurt." Three days later, Ali was in Istanbul with Wallace Muhammad, announcing his retirement: "Mark my words and play what I say fully. At the urging of my leader Wallace, I declare I am quitting as of now and from now on I will join in the struggle for the Islamic cause."

Ali's retirement lasted about eight months, or until another soft touch could be found for a healthy payday. This time it was Alfredo Evangelista, a Spaniard who, despite having fought professionally for only a year and a half, managed to last fifteen rounds of another lamentable Ali outing. A month later, Ali would marry Veronica Porsche, with whom he already had a nine-month-old daughter. They would honeymoon briefly in Hawaii, accompanied by Howard Bingham, Ali's best friend.

<hr />

"I'm so damn tired."

What with his new wife's taste for luxuries and the rising costs of providing for his entourage, Ali, whose own lifestyle had become relatively austere, needed to stay employed. The idea was to find some more easy (yet promotable) fights for

◆ UNUSUAL FIGHTS ◆

Between all his mainstream boxing matches, Ali was involved in two unusual matchups that verged on the ludicrous—one that never happened and one that sadly did.

On the heels of the loss to Frazier, Muhammad Ali briefly entertained the notion of a bout with basketball great Wilt Chamberlain. The match was Wilt's idea to begin with. A superb all-around athlete, he had gone so far as to work with Cus D'Amato, Floyd Patterson's trainer, in preparation for taking on Ali. Herbert Muhammad and promoter Bob Arum recognized the venture's obvious commercial value and presumably saw the 7-foot, 1-inch, 275-pound Hall of Famer as being of negligible ring risk to Ali. They arranged a meeting with Judge Fred Hofheinz, owner of the Astrodome, Ali, Wilt, and their lawyers. This was about as far as they ever got. According to Wilt, the deal fell through because of a disagreement over ancillary rights. But according to others, the fight was for all purposes quashed the moment Wilt entered the meeting room and was greeted by Ali, who couldn't resist yelling, "Timber!"

Billed alternately (and fraudulently) as the "War of the Worlds" and the "Martial Arts World Championship," the June 1976 "fight" between Muhammad Ali and Japanese wrestler Antonio Inoki proved little more than a lucrative lowlight of the champ's career. For a total six jabs thrown over fifteen rounds, Ali earned $6 million.

The bout's lack of action stemmed primarily from the rules, tilted in Ali's favor. Since Inoki was barred from delivering karate chops and flying kicks, he surprised Ali—who not wanting to trick the public, had refused to rehearse—by lying on his back and flailing away with leg sweeps the entire fifteen rounds, hoping to pull Ali to the canvas. By turn, Ali roamed the ring perimeter, imploring his opponent to get up and box and sometimes even kicking back like a poolside splasher. At one point Ali grabbed Inoki's foot and was nearly pulled down; at another, he ventured in too close and received a head butt to the groin. At no time did a punch ever land.

Probably the dullest event in sports history, it was watched by millions over closed-circuit television as well as by suckers in Tokyo who forked over $1,000 per ringside seat. Ali suffered ruptured blood vessels (from Inoki's constant leg whips) that would require hospitalization upon his return home.

decent purses (he'd earned $2,750,000 for Evangelista), the better to keep the coffers filled, the better to keep the legend alive. But as he grew older, that task became more difficult.

Now age thirty-five, Ali had defended his title nine times, had earned and spent a ton of money since the day he'd regained it three years earlier in the African jungle. The swan song loomed, but which fight would it be? Old fighters never know when to quit, went the old saw, and even the transcendent Ali proved to be no exception. So it was that he took a fight against Earnie Shavers, one of the most brutal heavyweight punchers of his era.

Just when ringsiders thought they'd seen the last of Ali the fighter, the proud and rugged Shavers would force the champion into yet another eleventh-hour show of heart. "Maybe he's had it," Angelo Dundee had suggested before the September 1977 Madison Square Garden fight. "Ali is a champ, he's a clown, he is anything he has to be to make money. But after a while, it gets thin." So, too, the punishment absorbed at the workplace. In the second round, Shavers landed an upside-the-head wallop that staggered Ali ("next to Joe Frazier, the hardest I ever got hit"). Shavers could have finished Ali then, had he realized the champ's predicament. Instead he fell for Ali's head-shaking con and chose to save energy for the later rounds. Ali survived further assaults, and by the fifteenth seemed hardly able to stand. "Fight hard until you die," he would later remember thinking. Which he did, with a brilliant from-the-grave attacking surge that left Shavers out on his feet at the final bell. "I'm tired," moaned Ali after his fifty-fifth win. "I'm so damn tired."

After the fight, Ali was once again urged by Pacheco and a few others to retire (though not by his sycophants, who never failed to tell him how good he looked). Laboratory results showed kidney damage, and doctors saw signs of neurological deterioration as well. For some years now, Ali had prided himself on his ability to "take" punches, the same punches he was happy to avoid as a younger fighter. There was little doubt that they'd taken their toll. The third Frazier fight, especially, had a detrimental effect that many believed marked the beginning of his neurological problems. Even Madison Square Garden matchmaker Teddy Brenner went so far as to announce the next day that he would never make Ali an offer to fight again. "The trick in boxing is to get out at the right time," he said, "and the fifteenth round last night was the right time for Ali."

In the six years since Ali had been exonerated by the U.S. Supreme Court, he'd gained gradual acceptance as a marketable celebrity. He appeared as himself in television commercials, had published his autobiography, and had starred in a film of his life appropriately titled *The Greatest*. There was a special edition of D.C. Comics that featured "Superman vs. Muhammad Ali," which sold for a dollar above the regular price. There were international service projects waiting, there was his ministry, his renewed pledges to serve Allah. There was talk of more acting roles. Retirement seemed imminent. Even Ali himself had grimly mumbled moments after the Shavers ordeal, "I'm through. I don't need anyone else to tell me."

Yet before that painful evening, Ali had also spoken of "two more lesser fights and then retirement—just give me twelve more months." When the possibility arose of such a "lesser" fight against 1976 Olympic champion Leon Spinks, Ali was interested. A match against a novice with but seven pro fights (the last a draw) was just the sort of made-to-order, low-risk payday a greatest-of-all-time almost thirty-six-year-old champion was looking for. If the kid made a good showing, the champ might even give him a rematch before riding off into the sunset.

1985

CHAPTER EIGHT

RETIREMENT

<hr />

For Ali at age thirty-six, boxing had become reduced to survival and playacting. When he wasn't miming, finger-pointing, gesturing, or trash-talking his way around his twenty-foot-square stage, he was busy fending off, clinching, ducking, and too often absorbing the relentless attack of disrespectful youth. Ali's fight game had become a sort of theater of the absurd, a bizarre clown act laced with elements of violence and fear, yet an act over which he still retained artistic control. Long gone were the shuffle, the flickering jab, the five-, six-, seven-punch combos that over two decades had backed up the daily claims to greatness; in their stead was an illusory mix of faded skills, that, strung together with guile and reputation, had somehow remained substantial enough to hold on to the heavyweight championship of the world.

Norton, Young, and even the journeyman Shavers had all

exposed Ali as an aging and seemingly disposable titleholder. In the boxing world, consensus dictated that Ali ought to hang up the gloves—he himself had admitted as much several times now. However, an offer of $3.5 million to stay in the cherished limelight with a February 1978 defense against bumbly Leon Spinks proved irresistible.

Spinks was an oddball of a challenger. The gap-toothed ex-marine, who had grown up idolizing Ali, now identified with Stallone's movie hero Rocky Balboa: "I damn near threw my hat at the screen when he knocked the man down. Tears ran down my face."

As a bullish amateur, he'd knocked out a favored Cuban for Olympic gold; as a novice professional, he showed disdain both for training and for increasing his limited ring knowledge. He possessed poor defensive skills, was slight for a heavyweight (6 feet, 1 inch, 195 pounds), and had looked awful in his last three fights. Few Las Vegas bookmakers thought enough of his chances even to post odds on their hometown affair.

Ali trained little for Spinks, although he had managed to starve himself down from 245 pounds to 225 by fight time. Miffed at what he considered too little press respect for the matchup (and Spinks' record), he announced that he would be silent until the fight, which did little to help sluggish ticket sales. (CBS reluctantly bought the fight, mostly because some 70 million viewers had tuned in to Ali-Shavers.) Uncharacteristically, Ali secluded himself in a Hilton suite with wife Veronica and their two daughters. One of his few prefight utterings was a poetic retort to a fan who had wished him luck: "Don't need no luck with The Duck."

But he would, as Spinks proved to be the latest in Ali's long line of forceful, awkward, and unflinching aggressors. Ali never took Spinks seriously, while the challenger, for all his camp escapades (midnight visits to poolrooms and discos), turned up in the best shape of his life. Carelessly, Ali blew the early rounds, talking, taunting, and seemingly hoping that the flailing Spinks would wear himself down. Spinks did tire midway, whereupon the soon-to-be-former-champion sprang to the attack. But while he could still conceive, Ali could not produce; age had dulled the timing, had dimmed the power. Giving as good as he got, Spinks easily survived Ali's slight resurgence, and the challenger gained a rightful split decision. As ripe as Ali had been for the taking, the result was still another tumultuous occurrence in an extraordinary athlete's extraordinary career. The champ had been slipping, for sure—but turn the crown over to Leon Spinks?

Afterward, the right side of his face swollen from the pounding, Ali confessed thinking during the fight that "this kid is a tough son of a bitch." And when somebody later expressed "surprise" at the loss, Ali shot back, "You're sitting down there ringside drinking beer and you think you're surprised? I was up in the ring getting my ass hit. You know I was surprised."

Otherwise, Ali was humble and gracious in defeat, as he had been on other similarly rare occasions. He praised his opponent and echoed a vaguely familiar refrain from what now seemed a distant past: "You can't die because you lose." He talked about taking a break for a few months, yet in the same breath mentioned Spinks giving him a rematch. "There's something telling me to leave," he added. "Then there's something telling me to try one more time. I used to get hungry when I lost fights. I don't know if I can be that way anymore."

Two days later, Ali was in Bangladesh, dedicating a sports stadium named in his honor. It was almost as though what happened in a Vegas ring had little or no bearing on Ali's international prestige. Three months after that, he traveled to the Soviet Union, where he was welcomed like a conquering hero, mobbed by crowds everywhere he went. By that time Leon Spinks was well into the aimless partying that marked his brief reign as champion.

After winning the title, Spinks was effusive in his praise for Ali. "I'm the best young heavyweight," he would say, "but he's still the greatest." Spinks readily agreed to a September rematch, prompting a bit of boxing politics that broke the hallowed line of heavyweight successors that reached back through Joe Louis and Jack Dempsey all the way to John L. Sullivan.

At the time, there were two major sanctioning bodies: the World Boxing Association and the World Boxing Council (today there are four "majors," as well as several smaller ones). Looking to get back in the heavyweight picture, promoter Don King prevailed on the WBC to strip Spinks of his title for having offered Ali a rematch before taking on Ken Norton, the WBC number one challenger. The group then declared Norton the interim champion, with the provision that he meet the winner of a Larry Holmes–Earnie Shavers "elimination bout." All three fighters had promotional obligations to King.

Ali cared little for official sanctioning; he knew that beating Spinks would make him the first three-time heavyweight champion, and that was enough for him. Within six weeks of the loss in Vegas, he was back to the gym and the roadwork, to thousands of extra miles and sit-ups, training with a vengeance and focus the likes of which he'd never known. "All my life I knew the day would come when I'd have to kill myself," he told *Sports Illustrated* two weeks before the fight. "To win all I need to do is suffer. I don't want to lose and spend the rest of my life saying, 'Damn, I should have trained harder.'"

In the weeks before the New Orleans rematch, the fast-living Spinks would disappear for days, only to be seen in a number of Bourbon Street dives. For Ali, everything was different this time. He was the motivated challenger, he was in his finest shape in years, and he was once again talking: "When I beat Sonny Liston, I shocked the world. When I joined the Muslims, I shocked the world. When I beat George Foreman, I shocked the world. I am from the House of Shock."

Given that Ali was a twelve-to-five betting favorite, his fabulous redemption over Spinks hardly shocked a world that had come to expect whatever minor miracles he might offer. Without even being a great fight, Ali-Spinks II was quite simply another testament to ring glory. As Ali himself had said days before the fight, "You can't write a movie no better than this."

Before some sixty-five thousand screaming fans in the Superdome and the second largest home television audience ever, Ali grabbed yet another slice of ring history, using the timeworn basic strategy of beating his opponent to the punch. There would be no foolishness, no rope-a-dope; this time Ali took his business to center ring with a jab that held Spinks at bay, with short, tight combinations that landed with purpose. By midfight Ali was well in control of a confused Spinks, who was little helped by a dozen seconds in his corner screaming conflicting advice. In the tenth round, out came the Ali shuffle; late in the fight the young champ, desperate for a knockout, was staggered repeatedly by counters as the "A-li! A-li!" chant echoed through the arena.

Ali joked with reporters after the fight that he'd done well for an old man. But he had looked old in winning what Dundee called a "beautifully sloppy" fight. Without actually coming out and saying it, Ali hinted at his imminent retirement. Over the next several months, he would ignore a number of fight offers,

LEON SPINKS

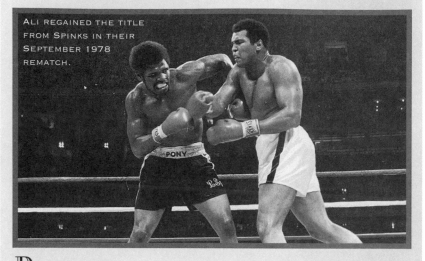

ALI REGAINED THE TITLE FROM SPINKS IN THEIR SEPTEMBER 1978 REMATCH.

Barely one month after he'd become the unlikeliest of heavyweight champions, Leon Spinks was arrested in the wee hours for driving down a wrong-way street in St Louis, with no driver's license and holding a small amount of cocaine. While not the first champion ever arrested, he may have gotten nabbed the soonest, which follows, given that his seven-month title span would be the shortest in history.

Many jokes were made at Leon's expense, even if he was, in his brief and shaky tenure, one of the sport's more affable titleholders. As Leon himself once said, "I was the nicest guy on the block. It was a mean block, but I was still a nice guy." Leon also claimed repeatedly that the Ali fight hadn't been his toughest, that many in his St. Louis street past had been far worse. As a scrawny adolescent, Spinks learned how to fight in the projects and was nicknamed "Mess-over" by the street toughs who regularly messed him over. "I'll never forget where I came from," he said after defeating Ali, "because I never want to go back."

Sadly, Leon Spinks would wind up a typical hard-luck boxing story—broke and destitute within a half dozen years after he'd rocked the world with his dazzling upset. While working as a bartender at age forty, he tried and failed in a pathetic comeback attempt in a seedy small-time fight promotion in the Midwest.

and on June 27, 1979, he officially called it quits. "Everybody gets old," he told reporters. "I'd be a fool to fight again."

~ ~ ~

"Boxing held me back."

At first, Ali seemed genuinely content away from the fight game. "I'm established now," he told *People,* on the set of "Freedom Road," a TV film he starred in as a fictitious slave who becomes a U.S. senator. "Boxing held me back. I'm free now." When questioned about his ability to handle "serious" roles, he laughed, "I been acting twenty years." He talked about endless speaking engagements ahead, about travel for his ministry ("world evangelism"), and about an international service foundation he was organizing called WORLD—World Organization for Rights, Liberty, and Dignity. "Service to others is the rent we pay for our room in heaven."

At Veronica's request, the Alis moved to an elegant mansion in the exclusive Hancock Park section of Los Angeles in 1979. But the L.A. scene more suited his wife than it did Ali, and gradually their marriage began to come apart. Special projects notwithstanding, away from the ring Ali was a man of simple pleasures, given to stuffing himself with pastries and watching cowboy and horror movies at home. Veronica was more interested in her growing social connections. One major strain on the marriage was whether the retired Ali could support her lifestyle, what with all of his other expenses.

Ali was estimated to have earned more than $50 million in professional boxing, but by 1979 much of that money was gone.

Taxes and poor investments had eaten up a large share, as had Ali's legendary generosity—not just his everyday handouts, but more significantly his reluctance to halt the out-and-out exploitation that plagued him in the latter part of his career.

The stories of Ali's munificence are legendary: his palming $100 bills to winos in the street; his rushing to save a Jewish retirement center with a $100,000 check after learning of its troubles on the evening news; his ritual donations to hospitals and charities; his everyday handouts to friends in trouble. In addition to that was his lassitude in dealing with those who dipped into his pockets and helped themselves: the crooks on the periphery of Ali's entourage who stole from him indiscriminately; the attorney who gambled away large sums held for Ali's taxes; the hustlers who signed Ali's name into bankrupt marketing deals. There were many individuals who played a hand in the withering away of Ali's finances. But even when criminal acts were obviously involved, Ali refused to press charges.

Most harmful were the half-baked and poorly managed schemes that both cost Ali money and kept him from earning rightfully from endorsements. "Champburgers" and "Champs Soda" were two such busts that never got off the ground. A possible lucrative tie-in with Converse fell through due to a prior shoe deal that never paid Ali a cent. Likewise a deal with Chrysler that was overridden by a ridiculous commitment to a doomed "Ali Motors" that was supposed to build a $35,000 sports car for sale in the Middle East. Then there was one Arthur Morrison, a man who, after finagling the right to use Ali's name on products, came up with Champion shoe polish and an ensuing trademark-infringement suit by Kiwi.

Of all the misuse of Muhammad Ali's name, perhaps the most bizarre was the embezzlement of $21 million in 1981 by Harold Smith, founder of Muhammad Ali Professional Sports.

With Ali lending his name in exchange for 25 percent of net profits, the organization was established to promote amateur and professional boxing. After outbidding rival promoters with extravagant purse offerings—sometimes bundles of cash dumped from pillowcases before prospective signees—Smith received a warm welcome in pro boxing. He claimed to have lost $10 million in his first year; no one seemed to wonder (or care) where the money came from.

Turned out the money was hot and actually belonged to Wells Fargo Bank. Through inside accomplices, Smith had had large amounts of money fraudulently transferred in what amounted to a near-brilliant computer scam. Smith served five years in prison. While his image was seriously tarnished, Ali was never implicated in any wrongdoing. "A guy used my name to embezzle $21 million," he laughed at a press conference. "Ain't many names can steal that much."

One year into his retirement, Ali was traveling the world over in his role as unofficial (and sometimes official) emissary for the Carter administration. After visiting India to raise funds for charities in early 1980, he flew to Africa to try to gain support for the United States–backed boycott of the Moscow Olympics. The trip was ill-conceived and ended embarrassingly for Ali when his appeals were rebuffed and his lack of understanding of Africa's complex political situation became evident. "If I'm to be looked at as an Uncle Tom or a traitor or someone against my black brothers," he said upon learning that Tanzanian president Julius Nyerere would not see him, "I want out, 'cause that's not my purpose." When he returned to America, he took a very hard look at a comeback offer to fight Larry Holmes for $8 million.

There were many people opposed to Ali's latest boxing comeback. Perhaps the most vocal was Dr. Ferdie Pacheco, who, while no longer in his corner—he'd had a falling out with Herbert Muhammad at the Shavers fight—best knew Ali's condition, having seen him deteriorate in the past couple of years. "There's no way for him to escape the attrition his body has undergone," he said at the time. "Even Muhammad Ali is subject to the laws of human nature."

❧ ❧ ❧

"... it's a no-win situation."

There were also those who would obviously benefit by Ali's return. Herbert Muhammad had plans for a $5 million mosque to be built in Los Angeles; Don King needed this title fight to extend his stranglehold on the heavyweight division; the entourage thirsted for any extension of Ali's career; and Ali himself, besides wanting to "shake up the world," could always use the scratch. "Where else can I make that kind of money in an hour?" he told Mike Phenner, his lawyer at the time.

To quell public outcry and placate the Nevada State Athletic Commission, Muhammad Ali took and passed a neurological exam at the Mayo Clinic. The "passing" of the exam was somewhat misleading, in that it placed him in basic good health, but for what should have been some obvious red flags regarding motor coordination. Those close to him knew he was slurring words, that his features were thickening, that he was slowing down—all signs of cumulative ring abuse. People around the gyms know even better than doctors when a fighter is in serious decline. The fight was signed for October 2, 1980.

The buildup to the Vegas bout was no different than others, and Ali, down to his gray hairs dyed over, skillfully conned many into believing he had a chance. With another torturous training schedule, he lost forty pounds of mostly belly fat and impressed camp visitors with his physique—never mind that much of his weight loss owed to amphetamines that would drain his energy. But most damaging of all was an apparently incorrect diagnosis made by Dr. Charles Williams, Herbert Muhammad's personal physician, that Ali had a thyroid condition. Dr. Williams prescribed one tablet of Thyrolar, a potentially lethal drug, and to make matters worse, Ali took three tablets instead of the one prescribed. The combination of age, ill effects from the drugs, and a sprightly and talented Larry Holmes left Ali with virtually no chance.

Since Ali had so convinced press and public that his well-shaped body would somehow translate to ring rebirth, the terrible beating he took in the desert came as a shock to the twenty-five thousand believers who attended it. With tank on empty from the start, Ali fell back on some tired gamesmanship—hanging to the rope with one hand, playing peekaboo behind gloves, while Holmes pounded away at his kidneys. It was apparent early on that the ex-champion had no starch to any of his punches, that he couldn't hurt Holmes, much less hit him. Once Herbert Muhammad had seen enough after ten pathetic rounds, he sent orders into the ring to stop the fight. Ali had thrown an estimated twenty-five punches the entire bout, though few of those landed. For his part, Holmes appeared to "carry" Ali in the fight's latter rounds, reluctant to tee off on his former idol, who was little more than a stationary target. "When you fight a man you admire and do what you have to do to him," Holmes said candidly afterward, "it's a no-win situation."

Sadly, Ali vowed to return, and he did, one year after his lifeless display against Holmes. "Forty is fun, because life has just begun," he quipped before fighting the ordinary Trevor Berbick in the Bahamas (few state commissions would at this point license Ali). "Age is mind over matter—as long as you don't mind it don't matter."

Little more than a footnote on a fight record that stretched back twenty-one years, the dismal, embarrassing ten-round loss to Berbick in December 1981 was at long last Ali's reluctant exit. It wasn't a very glorious way to go out—a low-rent promotion held in a decaying ballpark, with purse monies in doubt until the final minute. But the event's shortcomings— seedy dressing rooms, gloves forgotten for the main event, lack

With Lonnie, 1989.

of a bell and a timepiece (a cowbell and a stopwatch were eventually found)—in a way fit the falling-of-the-mighty scenario. "I think I'm too old," the flabby and tired Ali admitted afterward. "I was slow. I was weak. Nothing but Father Time. I know it's the end."

≈ ≈ ≈

"Too many people made me into an idol."

The next few years were empty and increasingly alone for the former champion. He appeared infrequently in public, his health continued to erode, and he seemed despondent living in the Los Angeles mansion—all as he and Veronica drifted farther and farther apart. In 1984 Ali, now forty-two, checked into a New York hospital and was diagnosed with Parkinson's syndrome—a group of symptoms similar, yet not identical, to the disease. The doctors were quick to insist that Ali did not suffer from "Punch-Drunk Syndrome" (PDS), yet they stopped short of stating that the ring punishment he'd absorbed over the years had nothing to do with his obvious motor deficiencies.

Ali and Veronica had signed a prenuptial agreement, yet Ali ordered his lawyers to ignore its stipulations when they were finally divorced in 1986. As a result, Veronica received a generous settlement and came away with more money and property than Ali did. It was clear that Ali would need someone to care for him in years down the road; in this respect, and many others, he had the good fortune to have at his side Yolanda (Lonnie) Williams, a childhood admirer of his (fourteen years his junior), who had moved to L.A. on her own in the early 1980s to help look after him. In middle age, Ali would at last find his perfect mate; he and Lonnie were married in 1986 and have forged a stable and loving union ever since.

With an M.B.A. from UCLA, Lonnie Ali would play a great role in helping straighten out and manage Ali's fragile finances. At the time of their marriage, ill-fated ventures were still associated with the champion's name. Five years later, the situation was greatly improved, all as Ali readily forgave those who'd defrauded him of millions of dollars—even those who would return to try their hand again.

In the early 1990s, Ali would come to terms with a condition that left him short on speech and movement, a condition his personal doctors were now admitting was a direct result of his "pugilistic experience." When not engaged in his arduous travel schedule, he was living comfortably on his farm in southwestern Michigan. He and Lonnie adopted a boy in 1990; at the same time, he remained close to his eight other children, who visited often. There would be ample income from business commitments ($1 million a year, according to a 1996 "60 Minutes" report), but Ali's daily focus tended more toward the spiritual and serving others than to making money. Every day, after rising and completing the first of his five daily prayer sessions, he would laboriously sign hundreds of autographs—to answer the endless requests that arrived by mail, as well as for the religious tracts that he passed out from day to day.

Under Louis Farrakhan, the Nation of Islam had turned back toward its separatist origins, and Ali now found himself aligned with the American Muslim Mission led by Imam Warithuddin Muhammad, another of Elijah Muhammad's sons. Ali no longer believed in Mr. Yacub's master plan and the like, but he would not totally reject Elijah either. "I think he was wrong when he talked about white devils," he told his biographer Thomas Hauser, "but part of what he did was make people feel it was good to be black."

In 1990 Ali was criticized for visiting Iraq on a peace mission before the Gulf War. Ultimately he helped convince Saddam Hussein to release fifteen American hostages. Well into his retirement, there were hundreds of trips for charities and causes—their frequency seemed to increase as he grew older. Ali travelled to impoverished Third World countries to help fight famine, to war-torn Bosnia to promote peace; he attended Cerebral Palsy benefits, United Fund dinners; he visited children's hospitals, women's prisons, old-age homes—in short, he went wherever he was asked. Unless he was too tired to travel, he went.

With Ali's many public appearances and his obviously debilitated state, it was common for people everywhere to pity what they saw as a stumbling, slurring shell of a once-riveting public figure, of the man who in their eyes once sparkled like no other athlete past or present. But Ali would have none of this, repeatedly stating that he wanted no one to feel sorry for him.

"Maybe this problem I have is God's way of reminding me and everybody else what's important," he said in 1991.

Given the splendidly lucid voice of decades past, it's understandable that people would be saddened by the vision of a tumbled icon. But to Ali, such sentiments seemed as personally unfair at age fifty as were the reactions to his religious beliefs at age twenty-five. It's a fitting paradox that he who once sought and found recognition as The Greatest would in another day say, "Too many people made me into an idol." But that die was cast long ago. No amount of acquired humility could keep the people from ignoring the fortunes or misfortunes of the one-and-"onliest" Greatest.

At the 1996 centennial Olympics in Atlanta, Muhammad

Lighting the flame at the centennial Olympiad, Atlanta, 1996.

Ali was chosen to ignite the Olympic flame. Millions world-wide watched as he took the torch from swimmer Janet Evans and steadied his ever-shaking arm to perform the ultimate ceremonial task. Ali stood trembling with Parkinson's, once again showing the world the courage and dignity of a champion for all times.

Afterward, Ali tirelessly signed autographs for hours in the Olympic Village. Athletes from all nations jockeyed to have their photos taken with him, and he obliged them all. At half-time of the U.S. basketball team's gold-medal victory, he was honored with a gold medal to replace his original, which had been lost or discarded somewhere through the years. And at the boxing arena, Ali beamed as he waved and blew kisses to ecstatic fans. "Ali! Ali!" they chanted, the same way they had some two decades earlier. "Ali! Ali!"

Subjective as they may be, comparative, over-the-years boxing ratings have fueled many a barroom argument. In 1973 four experts picked their top five in *Sports Illustrated:*

Teddy Brenner, Madison Square Garden matchmaker: 1. Joe Louis, 2. Rocky Marciano, 3. Muhammad Ali, 4. Joe Frazier, 5. Ezzard Charles

Jimmy Jacobs, fight film collector (and then future fight manager): 1. Muhammad Ali, 2. Joe Louis, 3. Rocky Marciano, 4. Gene Tunney, 5. Jack Dempsey

Nat Loubet, editor, *The Ring:* 1. Jack Dempsey, 2. Joe Louis, 3. Jack Johnson, 4. Muhammad Ali, 5. Jim Jeffries

Cus D'Amato, manager: 1. Joe Louis, 2. Rocky Marciano, 3. Muhammad Ali, 4. Jack Dempsey, 5. Ezzard Charles.

CHRONOLOGY

1942   January 17: Born in Louisville, KY
1954   October: Introduced to boxing by Joe Martin
        December: Defeats Ronnie O'Keefe in first
            amateur bout
1956   Wins his first title, a local Golden Gloves title
1958   Wins Louisville Golden Gloves
1959   Wins national light-heavyweight Golden Gloves title
1960   Wins second Golden Gloves title
        Wins gold medal in heavyweight division at Rome
            Olympics
        October 29: First professional fight. Win over
            Tunney Hunsaker in 6
        December: Hires Angelo Dundee as trainer
        December 27: TKO of Herb Siler in 4
1961   January 17: TKO of Tony Esperti in 3
        February 7: TKO of Jim Robinson in 1
        February 21: TKO of Donnie Fleeman in 7
        April 19: KO of Lamar Clark in 2
        June 26: Win over Duke Sabedong in 10
        July 22: Win over Alonzo Johnson in 10
        October 7: TKO of Alex Miteff in 6
        November 29: TKO of Willie Besmanoff in 7
1962   February 10: TKO of Sonny Banks in 4
        February 28: TKO of Don Warner in 4
        April 23: TKO of George Logan in 4

	May 19: TKO of Billy Daniels in 7

May 19: TKO of Billy Daniels in 7
July 20: KO of Alejandro Lavorante in 5
November 15: TKO of Archie Moore in 4

1963   January 24: KO of Charlie Powell in 3
Meets Drew Bundini Brown
March 13: Win over Doug Jones in 10
June 18: TKO of Henry Cooper in 5

1964   February 25: Wins heavyweight title by TKO
    of Sonny Liston in 7
Announces that he is a follower of Nation of Islam
Changes name to "Muhammad Ali"
May: Takes a month long trip to Africa
August 14: Marries Sonji Roi

1965   February 25: Malcolm X assassinated
May 25: KO of Sonny Liston in 1
November 22: TKO of Floyd Patterson in 1

1966   January: Divorces Sonji
February: Requests deferment from military service
March 29: Win over George Chuvalo in 15
May 21: TKO of Henry Cooper in 6
August 6: KO of Brian London in 3
August 23: Claims conscientious objector status to a
    special draft hearing
Autumn: Takes Herbert Muhammad as manager
September 10: TKO of Karl Mildenberger in 1
November 14: TKO of Cleveland Williams in 3

1967   February 6: Win over Ernie Terrell in 15
March 22: KO of Zora Folley in 7
April 28: Refuses to be inducted into the army
May 8: Indicted by a federal grand jury
New York State Athletic Commission suspends Ali's
    boxing license

	June: Convicted by a federal grand jury of unlawfully resisting induction
	August 16: Marries Belinda Boyd
1968	May: Ali's conviction upheld in Appeals Court
	June: Daughter Maryum is born
1969	November: Appears in the Broadway show *Big Time Buck White*
1970	U.S. Supreme Court decrees that conscientious-objector status is allowable on religious grounds alone, opening the way for Ali's return to the ring
	Twin daughters, Rasheeda and Jemillah, are born
	October 26: TKO of Jerry Quarry in 3
	December 7: TKO of Oscar Bonavena in 15
1971	March 8: Loses to Joe Frazier in 15. Frazier retains heavyweight title
	April 17: U.S. Supreme Court rules that all charges against Ali must be dropped
	July 26: TKO of Jimmy Ellis in 1
	November 17: Win over Buster Mathis in 12
	December 26: KO of Jurgen Blin in 7
	Son, Muhammad, Jr., is born
1972	January: Makes his hajj to Mecca
	April 1: Win over Mac Foster in 15
	May 1: Win over George Chuvalo in 12
	June 27: TKO of Jerry Quarry in 7
	July 19: TKO of Alvin (Blue) Lewis in 11
	September 20: TKO of Floyd Patterson in 7
	November 21: KO of Bob Foster in 8
1973	February 14: Win over Joe Bugner in 12
	March 31: Loss to Ken Norton in 12
	September 10: Win over Ken Norton in 12

	October 20: Win over Rudi Lubbers in 12
1974	January 28: Win over Joe Frazier in 12
	October 30: KO of George Foreman in 8 to regain the heavyweight title
	December 10: Visits the White House at the request of President Gerald Ford
1975	March 24: TKO of Chuck Wepner in 15
	May 16: TKO of Ron Lyle in 11
	July 1: Win over Joe Bugner in 15
	October 1: TKO over Joe Frazier in 14
1976	Daughter, Hana, is born
	February 20: KO of Jean-Pierre Coopman in 5
	April 30: Win over Jimmy Young in 15
	May 24: TKO of Richard Dunn in 5
	June 25: Exhibition with Antonio Inoki ends in draw after 15
	September 28: Win over Ken Norton in 15
1977	January: Divorces Belinda Ali
	May 16: Win over Alfredo Evangelista in 15
	June: Marries Veronica Porsche
	September 29: Win over Earnie Shavers in 15
1978	Daughter, Laile, is born
	February 15: Loses to Leon Spinks in 15, losing heavyweight title
	September 15: Win over Leon Spinks in 15 to regain heavyweight title
1979	June 27: Announces retirement from the ring
	Stars in TV-miniseries "Freedom Road"
	Travels to Africa to raise support for American boycott of the 1980 Olympics
1980	October 2: Loses to Larry Holmes by TKO in 11
1981	December 11: Loses to Trevor Berbick in 10

1984	Diagnosed with Parkinson's syndrome
1986	Divorces Veronica Porsche
	Marries Yolanda (Lonnie) Williams
1990	Visits Iraq on a peace mission during the Gulf War
1996	Lights the Olympic flame at the centennial Olympics in Atlanta, GA

BIBLIOGRAPHY

BOOKS

Ali, Muhammad, and Durham, Richard. *The Greatest*. New York: Random House, 1976.

Atyeo, Dan, and Dennis, Felix. *Muhammad Ali: The Holy Warrior*. New York: Fireside Books, 1975.

Braine, Tim, and Stravinsky, John. *The Not-So-Great Moments in Sports*. New York: Quill, 1986.

Chamberlain, Wilt. *A View From Above*. New York: Signet, 1992.

Conklin, Thomas. *Muhammad Ali: The Fight for Respect*. Brookfield, CT: Millbrook Press, 1992.

Cosell, Howard. *Cosell*. New York: Playboy Press, 1973.

Cottrell, John. *Muhammad Ali, Who Once Was Cassius Clay*. New York: Funk & Wagnalls, 1967.

Foreman, George, and Engel, Joel. *By George*. New York: Villard Books, 1995.

Frazier, Joe, with Berger, Phil. *Keep on Smokin'*. New York: Macmillan, 1996.

Fried, Ronald K. *Corner Men*. New York: 4 Walls 8 Windows, 1991.

Gorn, Elliott J., ed. *Muhammad Ali: The People's Champ*. Urbana, IL: University of Illinois Press, 1995.

Hauser, Thomas. *Muhammad Ali: His Life and Times*. New York: Simon & Schuster, 1991.

Lee, Martha F. *The Nation of Islam*. Syracuse, NY: Syracuse University Press, 1996.

Liebling, A. J. *A Neutral Corner*. Berkeley, CA: North Point Press, 1990.

Lipsyte, Robert. *Free to Be Muhammad Ali*. New York: Harper & Row, 1977.

Newfield, Jack. *Only in America: The Life and Crimes of Don King*. New York: William Morrow, 1995.

Olsen, Jack. *Black Is Best*. New York: Putnam, 1967.

Pacheco, Ferdie. *Muhammad Ali: A View From the Corner*. New York: Birch Lane Press, 1992.

Plimpton, George. *The Shadow Box*. New York: Lyons & Burford, 1977.

Ring Publishing. *The Ring Record Book*. Ring Publishing, 1986.

Schulian, John. *Writers' Fighters & Other Sweet Scientists*. Kansas City, MO: Andrews and McMeel, 1983.

Sheed, Wilfred. *Muhammad Ali*. New York: Thomas Crowell, 1975.

Sugar, Bert Randolph. *The 100 Greatest Boxers of All Time*. New York: Bonanza, 1984.

Torres, José. *Sting Like a Bee*. New York: Abelard-Schuman, 1971.

Wallechinsky, David. *The Complete Book of the Olympics*. New York: Penguin, 1984.

PERIODICALS

Boxing Illustrated

Esquire

The New York Times

The New Yorker

Newsweek

People

Playboy

The Saturday Evening Post

Sports Illustrated

Time

SOURCES

CHAPTER ONE

REFERENCES

Ali with Durham; Cottrell; Hauser; HBO; Lipsyte; Olsen;
  Sports Illustrated; Torres.

SOURCES

p. 3 *"The people know"*: *Sports Illustrated,* May 8, 1987.

p. 3 *"I ain't got no"*: Ali with Durham, p. 123.

p. 4 *"It is in light of "*: Hauser, p. 170.

p. 5 *"with a good body"*: Cottrell, p. 61.

p. 6 *"He'd walk way up"*: Olsen, p. 61.

p. 6 *"Our people were"*: Torres, p. 83.

p. 6 *"My family were real happy"*: ibid.

p. 8 *"If slaveholder [Henry] Clay's"*: Ali with Durham, p. 56.

p. 9 *"That's why I talk"*: Torres, p. 85.

p. 9 *"My father is a real"* and ensuing: ibid., p. 84.

p. 9 *"I couldn't get Emmitt"*: Ali with Durham, p. 35.

p. 10 *"I never got into any"*: Hauser, p. 17.

p. 10 *"sweet little fat"*: Torres, p. 86.

p. 11 *"He used to ask"*: Hauser, p. 17.

p. 11 *"Don't you hit my baby"*: ibid., p. 16.

p. 12 *"He was having a fit"*: HBO Muhammad Ali special.

p. 14 *"I realized it was"*: Lipsyte, p. 14.

p. 14 *"I'm Cassius Clay"*: ibid., p. 13.

p. 14 *"Almost from my first"*: Torres, p. 90.

p. 15 *"I started boxing"*: Hauser, p. 18.

p. 17 *"He really flattened Cassius"*: Olsen, p. 77.

p. 18 *"You would have thought"*: *Sports Illustrated,* September 25, 1961.

p. 18 *"Tell your readers"*: ibid.

p. 19 *"This is Cassius Clay"*: Lipsyte, p. 18.

p. 19 *"What's the matter"*: *Sports Illustrated,* October 14, 1967.

p. 20 *"Let's forget the Olympics"*: Cottrell, p. 22.

p. 21 *"Cassius really knew"*: Olsen, p. 76.

CHAPTER TWO

REFERENCES

Ali with Durham; Cottrell; Fried; Hauser; Lipsyte; *The New Yorker;* Pacheco; *Saturday Evening Post; Sports Illustrated;* Torres.

SOURCES

p. 23 *"I guess everybody do"*: *The Saturday Evening Post,* March 25, 1961.

p. 24 *"back home"*: ibid.

p. 25 *"I need top-notch"*: Cottrell, p. 33.

p. 25 *"He's a bum"*: *The Saturday Evening Post,* March 25, 1961.

p. 26 *"Let me give you"*: *Sports Illustrated,* March 3, 1963.

p. 27 *"The boy needed"*: Hauser, p. 34.

p. 27 *"The whole thing"*: Torres, p. 101.

p. 27 *"This is a new kind"*: Lipsyte, p. 28.

p. 28 *"This is my easiest"*: ibid.

p. 28 *"I'm gonna beat"*: Cottrell, p. 53.

p. 29 *"I'll go dancin'"*: Hauser, p. 37.

p. 29 *"What does this kid"*: Cottrell, p. 55.

p. 29 *"This is an age"*: ibid., p. 59.

p. 30 *"I said he would"*: Torres, p. 104.

p. 30 *"Am I scared of"*: *Sports Illustrated,* July 31, 1961.

p. 30 *"He boxed smart"*: Torres, p. 105.

p. 31 *"I saw 15,000 people"*: ibid., p. 104.

p. 31 *"A lot of people will"*: Pacheco, p. 50.

p. 32 *"embarrassed to get in"*: Cottrell, p. 59.

p. 32 *"When I've got"*: *Sports Illustrated,* September 25, 1961.

p. 33 *"really fell in love with"*: Cottrell, p. 62.

p. 33 *"What an old man"*: ibid., p. 63.

p. 34 *"Never send a boy"*: ibid., p. 82.

p. 34 *"Archie's been living"*: ibid.

p. 34 *"Liston in eight"*: ibid., p. 89.

p. 36 *"To make America"*: Ali with Durham, p. 70.

p. 36 *"It all started"*: Cottrell, p. 82.

p. 37 *"Clay comes out to"*: Hauser, p. 62.

p. 38 *"make Clay eat"*: Cottrell, p. 98.

p. 38 *"I talk very good"*: ibid.

p. 38 *"Why did these people"*: The New Yorker, March 30, 1963.

p. 39 *"I'm only here to"*: Torres, p. 117.

p. 39 *"After five rounds"*: Cottrell, p. 108.

p. 40 *"It's no big schmear"*: Sports Illustrated, May 24, 1965.

p. 41 *"If I was a person"*: ibid.

p. 41 *"I like him 'cause"*: Torres, p. 101.

p. 41 *"There's a right way"*: ibid.

p. 43 *"I'll demolish Sonny"*: ibid., p. 120.

p. 43 *"I hate to say"*: Sports Illustrated, July 1, 1963.

CHAPTER THREE

REFERENCES

Ali with Durham; Atyeo and Dennis; Braine and Stravinsky; Cottrell; *Esquire;* Gorn; Hauser; Lee; *The New Yorker;* Pacheco; *Playboy;* Plimpton; *Sports Illustrated;* Torres.

SOURCES

p. 46 *"Look at him"*: Cottrell, p. 113.

p. 46 *"The fight was"*: ibid., p. 116.

p. 46 *"You're next"*: Atyeo and Dennis, p. 38.

p. 46 *"Oink, oink!"*: Braine and Stravinsky, p. 64.

p. 46 *"a wise man can"*: Cottrell, p. 122.

p. 46 *"If I'm not asleep"*: Sports Illustrated, February 23, 1964.

p. 47 *"I don't know what"*: Pacheco, p. 70.

p. 47 *"I talk to reporters"*: Hauser, p. 55.

p. 47 *"The loudmouth from"* and ensuing: ibid., p. 68.

p. 48 *"A prizefight is like"*: Sports Illustrated, June 18, 1984.

p. 48 *"I think he died"*: ibid., February 4, 1991.

p. 49 *"I'm keeping a list"*: Plimpton, p. 87.

p. 49 *"It's my time to"*: Braine and Stravinsky, p. 66.

p. 49 *"Chump! Chump!"* and ensuing: reported in many sources.

p. 50 *"Liston is a bully"*: Pacheco, p. 75.

p. 50 *"At that moment"*: Torres, p. 129.

p. 50 *"Cut the gloves off!"*: Atyeo, p. 43.

p. 51 *"What are you talking"*: ibid.

p. 51 *"I want everybody to"*: Hauser, p. 78.

p. 51 *"I believe in Allah"*: Sports Illustrated, March 9, 1964.

p. 52 *"Where do you think"*: ibid.

p. 52 *"Black Muslims is a"*: Hauser, p. 82.

p. 52 *"After that, my"*: ibid., p. 89.

p. 53 *"The chickens have"*: reported in many sources.

p. 54 *"Do you think"*: Atyeo, p. 53.

p. 54 *"real American"*: Cottrell, p. 177.

p. 54 *"Clay will earn"*: Atyeo, p. 57.

p. 55 *"win back the title"*: Sports Illustrated, October 19, 1964.

p. 55 *"champion of segregation"*: Atyeo, p. 57.

p. 55 *"conned"*: ibid.

p. 55 *"After I beat him"*: ibid.

p. 55 *"I said I am"*: Playboy, April, 1964.

p. 55 *"I didn't know how"*: Atyeo, p. 57.

p. 56 *"Who are you"*: Hauser, p. 84.

p. 57 *"What he teaches"*: quoted in Gorn, p. 110.

p. 58 *"Do you have any"*: Hauser, p. 112.

p. 60 *"There was a limitless"*: The New Yorker, March 30, 1963.

p. 60 *"It seemed incredible"*: Plimpton, p. 87.

p. 60 *"the dirtiest in"*: Hauser, p. 120.

p. 60 *"I guess it's"*: ibid, p. 289.

p. 61 *"Having a Messenger"*: Ali with Durham, p. 196.

p. 61 *"If he'd stop all"*: Hauser, p. 125.

p. 63 *"Get up"*: reported in many sources.

p. 63 *"People said the first"*: Hauser, p. 128.

CHAPTER FOUR

REFERENCES

Ali with Durham; Atyeo; Cosell; Cottrell; Gorn; Hauser; Pacheco; *Playboy; Sports Illustrated.*

SOURCES

p. 65 *"I have nothing but"*: Sports Illustrated, October 19, 1964.

p. 66 *"deaf-dumb"*: Cottrell, p. 239.

p. 66 *"I'm gonna put him"*: ibid., p. 238.

p. 67 *"He had so much ability"*: Pacheco, p. 17.

p. 68 *"Ali, knock him out"*: Sports Illustrated, November 29, 1965.

p. 68 *"selfish and cruel"*: Atyeo, p. 62.

p. 68 *"A little boy"*: Hauser, p. 141.

p. 68 *"Patterson was fighting"*: Atyeo, p. 62.

p. 68 *"It's just this religion"*: Cottrell, p. 217.

p. 71 *"they told everybody"*: Hauser, p. 144.

p. 71 *"Man, I ain't got"*: Ali with Durham, p. 124.

p. 71 *"Cassius makes himself"* and ensuing quote: Hauser, p. 145.

p. 71 *"No Vietcong ever"*: Atyeo, p. 63.

p. 72 *"Any American who"* and ensuing: Hauser, p. 147.

p. 73 *"Clay in the United States"*: Sports Illustrated, April 11, 1966.

p. 74 *"Blood scares me"*: ibid., May 30, 1966.

p. 76 *"a champion fighting"* and ensuing: Atyeo, p. 67.

p. 76 *"People like Queen Elizabeth"*: Cottrell, p. 270.

p. 76 *"We know it's a"*: Hauser, p. 156.

p. 76 *"sincere in his"*: ibid, p. 155.

p. 77 *"Muhammad Ali knew"*: Cosell, p. 177.

p. 77 *"A mercurial man"*: ibid, p. 187.

p. 78 *"world rid of"*: Cottrell, p. 302.

p. 79 *"part of the promotion"*: Hauser, p. 162.

p. 79 *"I want to torture"*: Sports Illustrated, February 13, 1967.

p. 79 *"an open defiance"*: Hauser, p. 165.

p. 79 *"This may be the last"*: *Sports Illustrated,* March 3, 1967.

p. 80 *"civilized, respectable"*: ibid.

p. 80 *"He could write"*: *Sports Illustrated,* March 10, 1967.

p. 80 *"After I go"*: ibid., March 3, 1967.

p. 80 *"I am the tool"*: ibid.

p. 81 *"I refuse to be"*: Hauser, p. 169.

p. 81 *"My decision is a"*: ibid, p. 170.

CHAPTER FIVE

REFERENCES

Atyeo; *Esquire;* Hauser; Lipsyte; *The New York Times Magazine; Sports Illustrated; Time.*

SOURCES

p. 83 *"Allah okays the"*: *The New York Times Magazine,* May 28, 1967.

p. 84 *"Clean out my"*: Atyeo, p. 69.

p. 84 *"Step into a billion"*: ibid., p. 72.

p. 86 *"I still envy"*: *Sports Illustrated,* June 19, 1967.

p. 86 *"Let the man who"*: *Time,* March 8, 1971.

p. 88 *"They won't let me"*: Atyeo, p. 74.

p. 88 *"It don't matter"*: Author's interview with boxing historian Bert Randolph Sugar.

p. 89 *"did without and"*: Hauser, p. 185.

p. 89 *"Ali was providing a"*: ibid., p. 190.

p. 90 *"We worked through a"*: Atyeo, p. 74.

p. 91 *"if the money's right"*: Hauser, p. 194.

p. 91 *"Mr. Muhammad Ali"*: ibid.

p. 91 *"He sings with"*: ibid, p. 197.

p. 91 *"I'm through fighting"*: *Esquire,* May 1970.

p. 92 *"It might shock"*: reported in many sources.

p. 92 *"I don't want to"*: Frazier.

p. 93 *"He [Maddox] didn't know"* and ensuing quote: Atyeo, p. 76.

p. 94 *"moves like silk"*: *Sports Illustrated,* October 3, 1970.

p. 94 *"All of this leaves no"*: ibid.

p. 94 *"white buttons on"*: Hauser, p. 212.

p. 94 *"Quarry-sorry"*: *Sports Illustrated,* November 23, 1970.

p. 95 *"You took my title"*: Atyeo, p. 79.

p. 95 *"I want Joe Frazier"*: reported in many sources.

p. 96 *"I hated Ali"*: Hauser, p. 325.

p. 98 *"Joe's gonna come out"*: ibid., p. 222.

p. 98 *"The way they were hitting"*: *Sports Illustrated,* March 15, 1971.

p. 98 *"The punch that blew"*: ibid., April 5, 1971.

p. 98 *"Clay is good"* and ensuing: ibid., March 15, 1971.

p. 99 *"Oh, how wrong"*: Hauser, p. 233.

p. 99 *"Joe's the champ"*: Lipsyte, p. 96.

p. 99 *"If they fought a"*: Hauser, p. 232.

CHAPTER SIX

REFERENCES

Atyeo; Hauser; Plimpton; *Sports Illustrated.*

SOURCES

p. 101 *"When I beat Sonny"*: Hauser, p. 234.

p. 102 *"It's like a man's been"*: *Sports Illustrated,* August 26, 1971.

p. 103 *"Take him out"* and ensuing quote: ibid., November 29, 1971.

p. 104 *"It would have been"*: Atyeo, p. 90.

p. 104 *"Shinken ni yare"*: *Sports Illustrated,* April 10, 1972.

p. 105 *"Ain't this"*: ibid.

p. 105 *"I didn't want to"*: *Sports Illustrated,* August 10, 1972.

p. 106 *"a valid place for"*: Atyeo, p. 91.

p. 107 *"just another night"*: *Sports Illustrated,* December 4, 1972.

p. 107 *"My, there goes"*: Atyeo, p. 92.

p. 108 *"He's not going to get"*: *Sports Illustrated,* February 26, 1973.

p. 108 *"Winning took priority"*: Hauser, p. 252.

p. 109 *"revolutionizin'"*: *Sports Illustrated,* March 23, 1973.

p. 109 *"When I'm ready"* and ensuing: ibid., March 9, 1973.

p. 109 *"Took a broken jaw"*: ibid., March 23, 1973.

p. 109 *"I took a nobody"*: ibid., September 17, 1973.

p. 111 *"Joe Frazier's"*: reported in many sources.

p. 111 *"Can you believe"*: *Sports Illustrated,* February 4, 1974.

p. 113 *"I'm gonna beat your"*: Atyeo, p. 103.

p. 113 *"I can't let him"*: ibid.

p. 114 *"Places we go"*: ibid., p. 94.

p. 114 *"This is my"*: ibid.

p. 114 *"African friends"*: Plimpton, p. 236.

p. 114 *"I don't like fights"*: Hauser, p. 280.

p. 114 *"My opponents don't worry"*: ibid.

p. 115 *"This ain't nothing but"*: *Sports Illustrated*, November 11, 1974.

p. 115 *"manchild, con man"*: Hauser, p. 259.

p. 117 *"C'mon, champ"* and ensuing: *Sports Illustrated*, November 11, 1974.

p. 117 *"Don't I look"*: Atyeo, p. 109.

CHAPTER SEVEN

REFERENCES

Boxing Illustrated; Chamberlain; *Esquire;* Hauser; Lipsyte; Newfield; *Newsweek; The New York Times Magazine; Time;* Pacheco; Schulian; *Sports Illustrated.*

SOURCES

p. 119 *"secret wish to be seen"*: Hauser, p. 286.

p. 120 *"I'm like a little ant"*: *The New York Times Magazine*, June 29, 1975.

p. 120 *"You made a big mistake"*: Lipsyte, p. 106.

p. 120 *"We Muslims hate"*: *The New York Times Magazine*, June 29, 1975.

p. 121 *"He's a dirty ref"*: Hauser, p. 299.

p. 121 *"more transfusion than"*: *The New York Times Magazine*, March 24, 1975.

p. 121 *"I figured I held"*: *Time*, March 31, 1975.

p. 123 *"Talks black, lives"*: *Esquire*, March, 1991.

p. 123 *"That's one mean"*: author's interview with Mickey Duff.

p. 123 *"He didn't only"*: author's interview with Larry Holmes.

p. 123 *"Don King has been"*: author's interview with Bert Sugar.

p. 124 *"I want him"*: reported in many sources.

p. 125 *"You have a very"*: Pacheco, p. 30.

p. 125 *"I know celebrities"*: Hauser, p. 317.

p. 125 *"It'll be a thrilla"*: reported in many sources.

p. 125 *"It's real hatred"*: *Sports Illustrated*, September 29, 1975.

p. 125 *"each other"*: Hauser, p. 321.

p. 126 *"a little town"*: *Sports Illustrated*, September 27, 1976.

p. 128 *"Stay mean with"* and ensuing quote: ibid., October 13, 1975.

p. 128 *"They told me"*: *Newsweek*, October 13, 1975.

p. 128 *"It's all over"*: Pacheco, p. 141.

p. 128 *"If God ever calls"*: Hauser, p. 326.

p. 129 *"the closest thing to"*: *Sports Illustrated*, October 13, 1975.

p. 129 *"He fell and I"*: ibid., March 1, 1976.

p. 129 *"a boxer, a cute"*: ibid., May 10, 1976.

p. 130 *"The worst fight"*: ibid.

p. 130 *"I don't want to"*: ibid., May 23, 1976.

p. 130 *"I didn't go"*: Hauser, p. 333.

p. 130 *"I feed you niggers"*: *Sports Illustrated*, September 27, 1976.

p. 131 *"yellow nigger"*: *Time*, October 11, 1976.

p. 132 *"How long do you"*: *Sports Illustrated*, October 11, 1976.

p. 132 *"time to call it"*: Pacheco, p. 147.

p. 132 *"Mark my words"*: *Time*, October 11, 1976.

p. 133 *"Timber!"*: Hauser, p. 237.

p. 134 *"Maybe he's had it"*: Schulian, p. 9.

p. 134 *"next to Joe Frazier"*: Hauser, p. 346.

p. 134 *"Fight hard"*: *Sports Illustrated*, October 10, 1977.

p. 134 *"I'm tired"*: ibid.

p. 135 *"The trick in boxing"*: Hauser, p. 349.

p. 135 *"I'm through"* and ensuing quote: *Sports Illustrated*, October 10, 1977.

CHAPTER EIGHT
REFERENCES

Conklin; Hauser; *Newsweek; The New York Times Magazine; People;* Schulian; *Sports Illustrated; Time.*

SOURCES

p. 138 *"I damn near threw"*: The New York Times Magazine, January 29, 1978.

p. 138 *"Don't need no luck"*: Schulian, p. 15.

p. 139 *"this kid is a"* and ensuing quote: ibid, p. 16.

p. 139 *"You can't die"*: ibid.

p. 139 *"There's something telling"*: ibid, p. 17.

p. 140 *"I'm the best young"*: Time, February 27, 1978.

p. 140 *"All my life"*: Sports Illustrated, September 11, 1978.

p. 141 *"When I beat Sonny"*: Schulian, p. 18.

p. 141 *"You can't write a"*: ibid., p. 17.

p. 141 *"beautiful sloppy"*: Sports Illustrated, September 25, 1978.

p. 142 *"I was the nicest"* and ensuing: ibid., February 27, 1978.

p. 143 *"Everybody gets old"*: Hauser, p. 361.

p. 143 *"Boxing held me back"*: People, December 1978.

p. 145 *"A guy used my name"*: Hauser, p. 424.

p. 145 *"If I'm to be"*: Time, February 18, 1980.

p. 146 *"There's no way for him"*: Hauser, p. 403.

p. 146 *"Where else can I"*: ibid, p. 402.

p. 147 *"When you fight"*: Newsweek, November 13, 1980.

p. 147 *"Forty is fun"*: Sports Illustrated, December 21, 1981.

p. 149 *"I think I'm too old"*: ibid.

p. 150 *"I think he was wrong"*: Hauser, p. 97.

p. 151 *"Maybe this problem"*: Conklin, p. 92.

p. 151 *"Too many people"*: ibid.

p. 155 *Sports Illustrated* rankings—December 24, 1973.

PHOTOGRAPHY CREDITS

pp. iv, 113 courtesy of AP/Wide World Photos
pp. 1, 126 courtesy of Archive Photos
p. 2 courtesy of The Courier-Journal
pp. 3, 8 courtesy of The Courier-Journal
p. 17 courtesy of The Courier-Journal
p. 18 courtesy of AP/Wide World Photos
p. 21 courtesy of The Courier-Journal
p. 22 courtesy of FPG International
pp. 23, 42 courtesy of Archive Photos/Popperphoto
p. 31 courtesy of Photofest
p. 40 courtesy of Archive Photos
p. 44 © Thomas Hoepker/Magnum Photos, Inc.
pp. 45, 59 courtesy of The Courier-Journal
p. 48 courtesy of AP/Wide World Photos
p. 56 © Thomas Hoepker/Magnum Photos, Inc.
p. 64 © Thomas Hoepker/Magnum Photos, Inc.
pp. 65, 70 courtesy of Archive Photos
p. 69 courtesy of FPG International
p. 74 courtesy of AP/Wide World Photos
p. 77 courtesy of The Courier-Journal
p. 82 © Thomas Hoepker/Magnum Photos, Inc.
p. 83, 88 courtesy of AP/Wide World Photos
p. 85 courtesy of The Courier-Journal
p. 87 © Thomas Hoepker/Magnum Photos, Inc.
p. 96 courtesy of AP/Wide World Photos
p. 100 courtesy of Archive Photos/AFP
pp. 101, 116 courtesy of The Courier-Journal
p. 106 courtesy of The Courier-Journal
p. 110 courtesy of FPG International
p. 118 courtesy of Archive Photos
p. 119 courtesy of AP/Wide World Photos
p. 121 courtesy of AP/Wide World Photos
p. 122 courtesy of AP/Wide World Photos
p. 136 courtesy of Alfred/SIPA Press
pp. 137, 148, courtesy of Archive Photos/Consolidated News
p. 142 courtesy of AP/Wide World Photos
p. 152 courtesy of Michael Probst, AP/Wide World Photos

INDEX

Walcott, Jersey Joe 62
Ward, Gene 79
Warner, Don 33
Wells, Lloyd 127
Wepner, Chuck 120–21
Williams, Cleveland 78, 116
Williams, Yolanda 149–50
World Boxing Association 71,
  86, 140
World Boxing Council 140

World Community of al-Islam
  in the West (WCIW) 57
WORLD–World Organization
  for Rights, Liberty, and
  Dignity 143
Woroner, Murray 88
Young, Jimmy 129–30, 137
Youngblood (Muhammad),
  Wally 127

ACKNOWLEDGMENTS

I would like to thank the following people without whose invaluable help the writing of this book would not have been possible:

My wife, Dava, for good advice;

Thomas Hauser, for the generous permissions to quote from his book *Muhammad Ali: His Life and Times;*

Bert Randolph Sugar, for his continued role as professional boxing's "quote machine";

Chris Calhoun, for a strong ear;

Tom Dyja, for fine editorship;

South Country Library's head of research Nan Bunce and library assistants Diana Ivory, Kate Thomlinson, and Lia Vasquez-Gerrard, for all their help with sources and renewal requests;

The late A. J. Liebling, for inspiration;

and Muhammad Ali, for being The Greatest.

ABOUT THE AUTHOR

John Stravinsky specializes in the world of sports for publications such as *Sports Illustrated* and *The New York Times Magazine*. His previous books include *The Not-So-Great Moments in Sports* and *The Complete Golfer's Catalogue*.